GOOD HOUSEKEEPING

Microwave
HINTS

GOOD HOUSEKEEPING

Microwave
HINTS

An essential guide

Susanna Tee

EBURY PRESS LONDON

Published by Ebury Press
Division of The National Magazine Company Ltd
Colquhoun House
27–37 Broadwick Street
London W1V 1FR

First impression 1989

ISBN 0 85223 712 X

Editor Miren Lopategui

Computerset by MFK Typesetting Ltd, Hitchin, Herts
Printed and bound in Great Britain at The Bath Press, Avon

CONTENTS

INTRODUCTION

Whether you already own a microwave cooker, or are thinking of buying one, I am sure that you would like to be able to make full use of it. One thing I have discovered from travelling around the country and giving microwave cookery demonstrations, is that people are always interested in picking up hints on microwave cookery.

Here, then, gleaned from the *Good Housekeeping* cookery books, are many valuable tips learnt from years of experience and collected together in one book. All these – from wanting to know if you can dry herbs in the microwave to whether it is really save to use cling film – are presented in a simple question and answer format and listed in alphabetical order. The entries are then sub-divided so that you can quickly find the answer to your query. So, if, say, you want to know how long to allow to reheat a Christmas pudding, simply look in the section headed 'Christmas pudding'. Alternatively, if you want to know how to cook mashed potatoes in the microwave, look under 'Vegetables' and then 'Potatoes' to find the answer.

In addition to giving general tips, recipes illustrating the cooking technique of many specific dishes have been included. So if, for example, you want to know whether you can cook poppadums in the microwave, and the answer is yes, I've included the recipe too! In the past many people have asked me about cooking cakes in the microwave so I have also included hints on successful cake baking and a recipe for those of you wanting to make one for the first time.

As with any appliance, you have to use a microwave fully to get the best from it. *Good Housekeeping Microwave Hints* is packed with information on all aspects of microwave cooking. I hope all your particular questions have been answered so that you can get the best from your microwave cooker. Happy microwaving!

SUSANNA TEE

NOTE TO THE READER

Microwave Cookers

Unlike conventional ovens, the power output and heat controls on various microwave cookers do not follow a standard formula. When manufacturers refer to a 700-watt cooker they are referring to the cooker's POWER OUTPUT; its INPUT, which is indicated on the back of the cooker, is double that figure. The higher the wattage of a cooker, the faster the rate of cooking, thus food cooked at 700 watts on full power cooks in half the time as food cooked at 350 watts. That said, the actual cooking performance of one 700-watt cooker may vary from another with the same wattage because factors such as cooker cavity size affect cooking performance. The vast majority of microwave cookers sold today are either 600-, 650- or 700-watt, but there are many cookers which may be 400 and 500 watts.

In this book

HIGH refers to 100% full power output of 600-700 watts

MEDIUM refers to 60% of full power

LOW refers to 35% of full power

To follow the cooking instructions and recipes in this book, please see COOKER SETTINGS on page 51 to calculate the equivalent setting on your microwave cooker.

Combination Ovens

Like microwave cookers, combination ovens vary from one manufacturer to another and each oven varies in the way that you select the level of microwave energy and convected heat for combination cooking.

In this book I refer to either a HIGH, MEDIUM LOW or LOW microwave setting with temperatures ranging from 180 to 250°C. To discover the correct setting on your oven, refer to your oven manufacturer's handbook for the wattage of your microwave settings.

In this book

HIGH is equivalent to 600-650 watts (100% power)

MEDIUM LOW is equivalent to 195-240 watts (30-35% power)

LOW is equivalent to your lowest microwave setting

REMEMBER THAT THE MEDIUM LOW AND LOW SETTINGS MARKED ON YOUR OVEN MAY NOT BE THE SAME AS THOSE USED IN THIS BOOK.

If you cannot alter the microwave setting on your oven, always cook for the shortest stated time. If your oven has a series of programmed combined settings, check your handbook and choose the nearest appropriate setting, adjusting the cooking time accordingly.

A

ARCING

Q *What does the term 'arcing' mean?*

A When a metal reflects the microwaves and produces a blue spark, this is known as arcing. It occurs when a dish or utensil that is made of metal, or has any form of metal trim or gold or silver decoration, is used in the microwave. If arcing occurs the cooker should be switched off immediately as it can damage the cooker's magnetron (see page 80).

ARRANGING FOOD

Q *Does it matter how I arrange food in the microwave?*

A Yes. As a general rule, arranging food in a circle with the

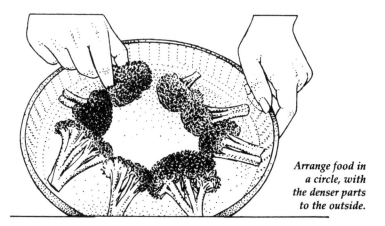

Arrange food in a circle, with the denser parts to the outside.

centre left empty will provide the best results because this will allow the microwaves to penetrate the food from the centre as well as the outside, thus ensuring even cooking. As microwaves are strongest from the outside edge, unevenly shaped foods such as chops, broccoli and asparagus should be arranged with the thinner parts or more delicate areas towards the centre.

AUBERGINE see VEGETABLES

AUTOMATIC PROGRAMMING

Q   *What is automatic programming on microwave cookers?*

A   This is a feature which allows more than one power setting to be programmed at once, so that a number of cooking sequences can be carried out on the one setting. For example, the cooker can be programmed to start off cooking the food at a HIGH setting, then to complete it on a LOW setting. Alternatively, you can arrange for it to come on at a set time and cook the food so that it is ready when you come home, or thaw food and then automatically switch to a hotter setting for cooking. As cooking in the microwave is so fast and should be watched most of the time anyway, automatic programming is purely an additional selling feature.

B

BABY FOODS

Q *Can I reheat baby foods in the microwave?*

A Yes, but greatest care should be taken to avoid making the food too hot. For this reason it is best to reheat it on a LOW setting. To heat glass jars of baby food, remove the lid, stir the food and always check the temperature before serving.

Q *Can I reheat babies' feed in the microwave?*

A Yes. The milk can be made up for the daily requirements, the right amount for each feed poured into sterilised bottles and kept in the refrigerator until needed. (All bottles and teats should be sterilised by the normal method with sterilising tablets, fluid or powder.) When required, unseal the bottle and place, opened, in the microwave, set on HIGH. (The heating time will obviously depend on the quantity of milk being heated.) The outside of the bottle will feel cooler than the feed, therefore always check the temperature of the feed before offering it to the baby.

BACON see MEAT

BAKED BEANS

Q *Can I heat baked beans in the microwave?*

A Yes. Tip the baked beans on to buttered toast and cook on HIGH for 1 minute or until hot. An instant snack without a saucepan or any mess!

BASKETS

Q *Is it true that it's safe to put wood and straw baskets in the microwave?*

A Yes. They can be used for briefly reheating foods such as bread rolls. If they are used for a long time, however, they are likely to char. (See BREAD ROLLS page 18).

BISCUITS

Q *Is it possible to cook biscuits in the microwave?*

A Few biscuits are suitable for cooking in a microwave because they can only be cooked in small batches and also often need to be turned over. Also, they will generally not be crisp. Stickier types, such as flapjacks, which are cooked in one piece and then cut into bars, however, are ideal. If you are making biscuits in your microwave for the first time be sure to follow a recipe that is especially written for microwave cooking. Here is a recipe for you to try.

FLAPJACKS

MAKES 16

75 g (3 oz) butter or margarine
50 g (2 oz) light soft brown sugar
30 ml (2 tbsp) golden syrup
175 g (6 oz) porridge oats

1 Grease a shallow 12.5 x 23 cm (5 x 9 inch) dish.

2 Put the butter or margarine, sugar and syrup into a large bowl. Cook on HIGH for 2 minutes until the sugar has dissolved, stirring once. Stir well then mix in the oats.

3 Press the mixture into the dish. Stand on a roasting rack and cook on HIGH for 2-3 minutes until firm to the touch.

4 Leave to cool slightly, then mark into sixteen bars. Allow to cool completely before turning out of the dish.

BLANCHING

Q *Can I blanch vegetables in the microwave before freezing them?*

A Yes. A maximum of 450 g (1 lb) prepared vegetables can be blanched at one time. To blanch vegetables in the microwave, put the vegetables and 45-60 ml (3-4 tbsp) water in a large bowl. Cover and cook on HIGH for 2 minutes. Stir and cook on HIGH for a further 1-2 minutes until all the vegetables are hot. Drain and plunge the vegetables into ice-cold water then drain and pack in polythene bags.

Q *Can I blanch nuts in the microwave?*

A Yes. See NUTS page 93.

BOILING

Q *How do I boil food in the microwave?*

A As in conventional cooking, boiling is the method of cooking foods such as vegetables, pasta and rice in boiling liquid. However, because microwave cooking is a moist form of cooking, less liquid is needed than in conventional cooking. Never attempt to boil eggs in the microwave as they will explode.

Here are some hints for successful boiling:

- Use a large container. Never fill any bowl more than two thirds full. This allows liquids to boil without spilling over the top and allows space for stirring.

- Cover the container with a large plate or a lid. Cling film is no longer recommended for use in a microwave (see page 55).

- If you require more than 300 ml (½ pint) water (for example when cooking rice, pasta and pulses), then it is quicker to boil the water in the kettle before adding it to the bowl.

- Cut vegetables into uniformly sized pieces so that they cook evenly.

BREAD

Q *Can I cook bread in the microwave?*

A Yes. But it will not have the characteristic crisp crust of conventionally baked bread because, when bread is cooked in a microwave, moisture is drawn to the surface and prevents it from becoming crisp. However, this can easily be overcome by browning the loaf under a hot grill after cooking. Using wholemeal flour will also help to give the bread colour. As a rough guide a 450 g (1 lb) loaf will take about 6 minutes to cook (always stand on a roasting rack). Leave to stand for 10 minutes before turning out. Soda bread works very well: here is a recipe.

SODA BREAD

MAKES ONE 450 g (1 lb) LOAF
450 g (1 lb) plain wholemeal flour
5 ml (1 level tsp) salt
5 ml (1 level tsp) bicarbonate of soda
15 g (½ oz) butter or margarine
10 ml (2 level tsp) cream of tartar
5 ml (l level tsp) dark soft brown sugar
about 300 ml (½ pint) milk

1   Grease a microwave baking tray or a large flat plate. Mix the flour, salt and bicarbonate of soda in a large bowl and rub in the butter or margarine until the mixture resembles fine breadcrumbs.

2   Add the cream of tartar and sugar to the milk and stir until dissolved. Add to the flour mixture and mix to form a soft dough, adding a little more milk if necessary.

3   Knead the dough on a lightly floured surface until it is firm and smooth and there are no cracks.

4   Flatten out the dough to a round about 18 cm (7 inches) in diameter and place it on the prepared tray or plate.

5 Brush the surface of the dough with a little milk and mark a deep cross on the top with a knife. Sprinkle a little flour on top.

6 Stand on a roasting rack and cook on HIGH for 8-9 minutes or until the bread is well risen and the surface looks dry, turning the dish two or three times during cooking. Turn the bread over and cook on HIGH for a further 1–1½ minutes or until the bottom looks dry. Leave to stand for 2-3 minutes, then serve immediately. This bread is best served warm.

Q *Can I warm flour for breadmaking in the microwave?*

A Yes. Put the flour in a large, heatproof bowl and make a well in the centre. Cook on HIGH for 2-3 minutes or until just warm.

Q *Can I prove bread dough in the microwave?*

A The microwave can be used to speed up the rising process of bread dough. It should, however, be watched all the time to prevent the dough from becoming too hot and therefore killing the yeast. To prove bread dough in the microwave, put the dough in a large bowl, cover with a clean tea-towel and cook on HIGH for 15 seconds then leave to stand for 5 minutes. Repeat the cooking and standing five or six times until the dough springs back when pressed lightly with the fingertips.

Q *What is the best way to thaw bread in the microwave and how long does it take?*

A Place the bread on absorbent kitchen paper (remove as soon as thawed to prevent sticking) to absorb the moisture of thawing bread. For greater crispness, place the bread and the paper on a microwave rack to allow the air to circulate underneath. Follow the chart overleaf for thawing times.

B

BREAD

Type	Quantity	Time on LOW or DEFROST Setting	Notes
Loaf, whole	1 large 1 small	6–8 minutes 4–6 minutes	Uncover and place on absorbent kitchen paper. Turn over during thawing. Stand for 5–15 minutes.
Loaf, sliced	1 large 1 small	6–8 minutes 4–6 minutes	Thaw in original wrapper but remove any metal tags. Stand for 10–15 minutes.
Slice of bread	25 g (1 oz)	10–15 seconds	Place on absorbent kitchen paper. Time carefully. Stand for 1–2 minutes.
Bread rolls, tea-cakes, scones, crumpets etc.	2 4	15–20 seconds 25–35 seconds	Place on absorbent kitchen paper. Time carefully. Stand for 2–3 minutes.

Bread rolls

Q *Can I warm bread rolls in the microwave?*

A Yes. Place the bread rolls in a wicker basket, lined with a paper napkin if liked. Cook on HIGH for 30-45 seconds until warm. Do not overcook or the rolls will become hard.

Breadcrumbs

Q *Is it possible to dry fresh breadcrumbs in the microwave?*

A Yes. After making the breadcrumbs in a food processor or blender, spread them on to a plate lined with absorbent kitchen paper and cook on HIGH until they are dried, stirring occasionally. (75 g (3 oz) breadcrumbs will take 3-4 minutes.) Cool and store in a polythene bag.

18

BROWNING DISHES AND GRIDDLES

Q *What are browning dishes and griddles?*

A These are dishes that are made of a special material which absorbs microwave energy. They are heated empty in the microwave cooker for 8-10 minutes, or according to the manufacturer's instructions, during which time they get very hot. The food is then placed on the hot surface and is immediately seared and browned.

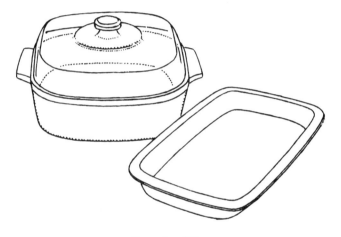

Browning dishes

Q *How do you use a browning dish or griddle in the microwave?*

A Follow the tips below:
   - Heat the empty browning dish or griddle on HIGH for 5-8 minutes or according to the manufacturer's instructions.

   - Use oil for a crisp, brown surface, but only a maximum of 30 ml (2 tbsp).

   - Do not remove the browning dish or griddle from the cooker as its temperature will quickly lower. Add the oil and food quickly to the dish as it sits inside the microwave.

- Use oven gloves when removing the dish from the cooker as it becomes very hot.
- Use tongs when repositioning food so that the fat is less likely to splatter.
- When turning food over, place it on a different part of the dish so that the maximum heat from the dish is used.

BROWNING ELEMENT

Q *What is a browning element?*

A This device works in the same way as a conventional grill and is especially useful when the microwave is the main cooking appliance since there is then no need to transfer a dish to a conventional grill for browning. A browning element is obviously not necessary for those who already have a grill.

BURNING

Q *Is it possible to burn yourself in a microwave cooker?*

A No, because the microwave energy is automatically switched off as soon as you open the cooker door, and the cooker itself does not get hot. Dishes and bowls, however, can get hot due to the conduction of heat from the food being cooked in them and browning dishes become very hot when they are heated, so never remove any of these from the cooker without using oven gloves.

BUTTER

Q *Can I soften butter in the microwave so that it reaches a spreading consistency?*

A Yes. This is very useful when you want to spread butter that you have taken straight from the refrigerator! To soften butter, cook on LOW for 30 seconds to 1 minute until a spreading consistency is reached.

BUTTER

Q *What is the best way to melt butter in the microwave?*

A To melt butter, cut quantities over 25 g (1 oz) into cubes. Put the butter in a small bowl and cook on HIGH until melted. (15 g (½ oz) butter takes about 30 seconds; 25 g (1 oz) about 45 seconds; 50-75 g (2-3 oz) about 1 minute; 100 g (4 oz) 1½-2 minutes.)

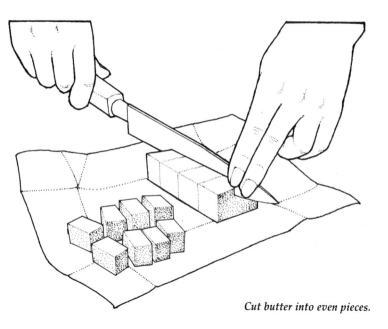

Cut butter into even pieces.

C

CAKES AND TEABREADS

Q *How should I prepare the container for cooking a cake in the microwave?*

A Cakes baked in a plastic container will not need greasing unless the mixture you are using contains only a small amount of fat. Other containers, however, should be greased and the base of larger containers lined with greaseproof paper. Avoid flouring dishes as this will produce an unpalatable coating on the cake.

Q *What do you consider is the best container for cooking a cake in the microwave?*

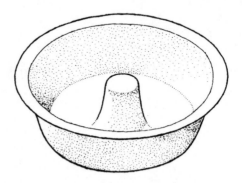

Ring moulds are ideal for microwave cooking as microwaves can reach the food from the inside as well as the outside.

A A microwave ring mould is best, since it allows penetration of microwaves from all sides. This means that the cake will cook evenly, with no uncooked centre! (see RING MOULD, page 111)

Q *Please can you give me some hints for baking cakes in the microwave?*

A • Mixtures should be a softer consistency than when baked conventionally. Add an extra 15 ml (1 tbsp) milk for each egg used.

Add milk to make a dropping consistency.

• Make sure the containers you use are large enough, as mixtures rise during microwave cooking. Containers should not be more than half-full of uncooked mixture.

• Large cakes are better if cooked in a ring mould, otherwise the centre will not be cooked.

• Cook small cakes in small paper cases – use two per cake for extra support.

- When cooking a number of small cakes arrange them in a circle about 5 cm (2 inches) apart for even cooking: do not put a cake in the centre. This ensures even penetration of the microwaves and therefore even cooking.

- Cakes that are not cooked in a ring mould should be raised on a microwave roasting rack or a trivet during cooking so that the microwaves can penetrate the cake from all sides.

- Even if the microwave has a turntable or stirrer, cakes that rise unevenly should be repositioned during cooking to ensure even cooking.

- Remove cakes from the cooker when they are still moist on top then leave for the standing time recommended in the recipe. This will prevent overcooking.

Q *How do you test when a cake is cooked in the microwave?*

A Cakes should be removed from the cooker while still moist in areas on the surface (normally they would be considered slightly underdone), then left for the time recommended in the recipe. During the standing time the cooking will be completed by the conduction of heat. Teabreads, which are firmer mixtures, should look dry on the surface.

Q *I've never made a cake in the microwave before. Do you have a recipe that I could try for the first time ?*

A Yes, this is the quickest, simplest cake in the world to make! It's made by the all-in-one method, mixed in one bowl and is failproof! Not only that, it looks and tastes delicious.

CHOCOLATE SWIRL CAKE

SERVES 8
100 g (4 oz) soft tub margarine *60 ml (4 tbsp) milk*
100 g (4 oz) caster sugar *175 g (6 oz) self raising flour*
2 eggs *10 ml (2 level tsp) cocoa powder*

Reposition during cooking.

1   Grease a 1.6 litre (2¾ pint) ring mould and line the base with a ring of greaseproof paper.

2   Put all the ingredients except the cocoa powder in a bowl and beat together until pale and fluffy.

3   Spoon half of the mixture, leaving gaps between each spoonful, into the base of the ring mould.

4   Beat the cocoa into the remaining mixture, then spoon into the spaces left in the ring mould.

5   Draw a knife through the cake mixture in a spiral to make a marbled effect and level the surface.

6   Cover with absorbent kitchen paper and cook on HIGH for 4–5 minutes until well risen and firm to the touch. Leave to stand for 10 minutes, then turn out and leave to cool on a wire rack.

Q *How can I overcome the problem of cakes not browning in the microwave?*

A To overcome this problem, either use cocoa powder, chocolate, brown sugar, spices or brown flour in the mixture or add an icing to the cooked cake.

Q *I've tried making cakes and teabreads in the microwave but never with much success. Can you tell what I might be doing wrong?*

A These hints will hopefully tell you where you are going wrong.

Cake or teabread is dry:
- You have overcooked the cake. When in doubt about timings, it's always best to underbake. You can always put the mixture back in the microwave for a few seconds, if necessary. (See *How do you test when a cake is cooked in the microwave?* page 24).

- Not enough liquid added. Mixtures should be more moist than conventional cakes; add an extra 15–30 ml (1–2 tbsp) milk for every egg.

- Mixture should have been covered during cooking. A cover helps retain moisture.

Uncooked circle of mixture on base of cake or teabread:
- The bottom of a deep cake or teabread cooks most slowly. Cook standing on a roasting rack or upturned plate. Return partly uncooked cakes to the cooker inverted on to a plate and cook for 1–3 minutes on HIGH. Be careful not to overcook – you should remove the mixture as soon as it has set. A dark circle of mixture will still be visible after extra cooking but will not show once the cake is filled and decorated.

- Cooker setting incorrect (see page 51).

One large patch of a cake or teabread burned:
- Cooker has a hotspot. Turn cakes frequently during cooking.

Burned patches throughout a cake or teabread:
- Lumpy sugar added to the mixture. The lumps of sugar get very hot during cooking and result in burned patches.

- Too much dried fruit added. Dried fruit contains a high proportion of sugar and has the same effect as lumps of sugar. If using your own recipe, cut down on the amount of fruit. Alternatively, try washing the fruit before coating it in flour. This should cut down on very sticky surfaces.

- Too much sugar in the cake mixture. If adapting your own cake or teabread recipe it may be unsuitable.

Teabread dry at ends but moist in centre:
- Cooking time too long. Watch teabreads during cooking: the ends will cook much faster than the centre. When the centre rises, test to see if cooked.

- Power level incorrect. Some teabreads benefit from being cooked on a MEDIUM setting.

- Dish not turned during cooking. If the teabread is rising unevenly, it means that it is cooking unevenly. Watch during cooking and turn if necessary.

Q *How should I thaw cakes in the microwave and how long does it take?*

A To absorb the moisture of thawing cakes, place them on absorbent kitchen paper (remove as soon as they are thawed to prevent sticking). For greater crispness, place the baked goods and the paper on a microwave rack to allow the air to circulate underneath. Follow the chart overleaf for thawing times.

CAKES AND TEABREADS

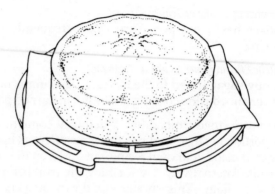

Place the cakes on absorbent kitchen paper then stand on a rack.

Type	Quantity	Time on LOW or DEFROST Setting	Notes
Cakes	2 small 4 small	30–60 seconds 1–1½ minutes	Place on absorbent kitchen paper. Stand for 5 minutes.
Sponge cake	450 g (1 lb)	1–1½ minutes	Place on absorbent kitchen paper. Test and turn after 1 minute. Stand for 5 minutes.
Jam doughnuts	2 4	45–60 seconds 45–90 seconds	Place on absorbent kitchen paper. Stand for 5 minutes.
Cream doughnuts	2 4	45–60 seconds 1¼–1¾ minutes	Place on absorbent kitchen paper. Check after half the thawing time. Stand for 10 minutes.
Cream éclairs	2 4	45 seconds 1–1½ minutes	Stand for 5–10 minutes. Stand for 15–20 minutes.
Choux buns	4 small	1–1½ minutes	Stand for 20–30 minutes.

Q *Is it necessary to cover cakes when cooking them?*

A Covering cakes with a plate during cooking keeps them moist but they are then similar in texture to a sponge pudding. A light covering is therefore the answer so the best thing to use is a double thickness of absorbent kitchen paper. Teabreads do not need covering because they do not require moist cooking.

CASSEROLES AND STEWS

Q *Can I cook a casserole or stew in the microwave?*

A Not really. Conventionally cooked casseroles and stews depend on long, slow cooking to tenderise tough cuts of meat and allow the flavours of the vegetables and herbs to combine. For this reason, there is little point in using the microwave for stews, other than those with ingredients which do not need tenderising (for example, those using poultry, vegetables and tender cuts of meat).

CAULIFLOWER, see VEGETABLES

CHEESE

Q *Can you give me some hints for cooking cheese dishes in the microwave?*

A • Whenever possible, add cheese at the end, rather than at the beginning, of cooking a dish. If overcooked it will become tough and rubbery.

  • Cheese will cook more evenly if grated rather than sliced or diced.

  • Use the microwave cooker for speedily cooking the basic ingredients for *au gratin* and cheese-topped savoury dishes then brown and crisp the surface under a conventional grill.

CHEESE

Q *Is it true that you can ripen cheese in the microwave?*

A You can, but please only do so if you are desperate! Put the cheese – a soft cheese such as Brie is most suitable – in the microwave and cook on LOW for 30 seconds. Then leave to stand for a few minutes before serving.

Q *Can I make cheese on toast in the microwave?*

A Although it's not the same as grilled cheese on toast, it is possible to make something similar and is a useful tip to know if you don't own a grill. Simply toast the bread normally (you do need a toaster!) then place on a large, flat plate and cover with thin slices of cheese. Cook on HIGH for 30 seconds–1 minute or until the cheese melts.

CHESTNUTS

Q *Is it true that you can roast chestnuts in the microwave?*

A Yes. To roast chestnuts, slit the skins with a sharp knife and cook on HIGH for 3 minutes per 225 g (8 oz).

Break chocolate into small pieces.

CHOCOLATE

Q *What's the best way to melt chocolate in the microwave?*

A Break the chocolate into small pieces (unless using chocolate chips), and cook on LOW just until the chocolate is soft
and glossy on top. (As a guide, 100 g (4 oz) cooking chocolate takes about 4 minutes on LOW.) The melting times will
vary according to the material and shape of container used,
so it is advisable to check every minute during melting. Take
care not to overcook because chocolate burns easily in the
microwave. Remove from the cooker and stir until melted.

CHRISTMAS PUDDING

Q *Can I cook a Christmas pudding in the microwave?*

A Yes. A Christmas pudding can be cooked in a microwave
but because the traditional Christmas pudding recipe contains a high proportion of sugar, dried fruits, fat and alcohol, all of which attract microwave energy and quickly reach
a high temperature, it means great care must be taken not to
overcook and possibly burn the pudding. As this may be
potentially dangerous Christmas pudding should be
watched during cooking. However, a Christmas pudding
can be cooked in only 45 minutes in the microwave instead
of 6–8 hours by conventional cooking, and you do not need
a saucepan of boiling water that has to be continually re-
plenished. If, therefore, you are adapting your favourite
Christmas pudding recipe, only add 30 ml (2 tbsp) of the
alcohol suggested and replace the remaining liquid with
milk or orange juice. Additional liquid should also be added
to keep the pudding moist: allow an extra 15 ml (1 tbsp) milk
for each egg added. Because a pudding cooked in a microwave does not have long, slow cooking, it will not keep like
the traditionally cooked pudding and should be eaten fairly
soon after making. Store for up to 2–3 weeks in a cool place.
The recipe is overleaf.

CHRISTMAS PUDDING

SERVES 8

450 g (1 lb) mixed dried fruit
175 g (6 oz) stoned prunes
450 ml (¾ pint) orange juice
100 g (4 oz) plain flour
1.25 ml (¼ level tsp) freshly grated nutmeg
1.25 ml (¼ level tsp) ground cinnamon
2.5 ml (½ level tsp) salt
75 g (3 oz) fresh breadcrumbs
100 g (4 oz) shredded suet
100 g (4 oz) dark soft brown sugar
25 g (1 oz) blanched almonds, chopped
finely grated rind of ½ lemon
30 ml (2 tbsp) sherry
2 eggs, beaten

1 Line the base of a 1.3 litre (2½ pint) pudding basin with a circle of greaseproof paper.

2 Put the dried fruit, prunes and orange juice in a large bowl and mix well together. Cover and cook on HIGH for 20 minutes until the fruit is plump and the liquid absorbed. Leave to cool.

3 Add remaining ingredients to fruit mixture and mix well. Spoon mixture into prepared basin, pushing down well.

4 Cover the bowl with a plate and cook on MEDIUM for 25–30 minutes until the top is only slightly moist.

5 Leave to stand covered for 5 minutes before turning out on to a warmed serving plate.

Q *Can I reheat a Christmas pudding in the microwave and if so, how long should I allow?*

A Christmas puddings containing a large quantity of alcohol or those that have previously been flambéed are unsuitable for reheating in a microwave because of the risk of them catching fire. If, however, neither of these applies, this is how you do it:

1   Remove all the wrappings and basin from the pudding. Put the pudding on an ovenproof serving plate, cut into the required number of portions and pull apart so that there is a space in the centre.

2   Place a small tumbler of water in the centre. This introduces steam and helps to keep the pudding moist. Cover with a large upturned bowl.

3   Cook on HIGH for 2–3 minutes, depending on the size of the pudding, or until hot.

4   Remove the cover and glass and reshape the pudding with the hands. Decorate with a sprig of holly and serve.

5   To reheat an individual portion of Christmas pudding, put on a plate and cook, uncovered, for 1–1½ minutes until hot.

CLEANING

Q   *What's the best way to clean a microwave cooker?*

A   It is important to clean the interior each time you use it as any spillage will absorb microwave energy and slow down the cooking the next time the cooker is used. Cleaning is easy – simply wipe with a damp cloth. Should the cooker walls become heavily soiled, place a bowl of water in the cooker and heat on HIGH to boiling point. The steam that is produced will soften any stubborn particles. Do not use abrasive cleaners as they will damage the surfaces.

CLING FILM

Q   *Is it safe to use cling film in the microwave? I've heard that it isn't.*

A   See COVERING, page 55.

COCONUT

Q *Is it possible to brown desiccated coconut in the microwave?*

A Yes. Put the coconut in a roasting bag and cook on HIGH for 5 minutes or until brown.

COFFEE

Q *Can I reheat fresh coffee that has gone cold, in the microwave?*

A Yes. Pour the coffee into cups or mugs and cook on HIGH. (1 cup will take 1½ minutes; 2 cups will take 2–3 minutes; 4 cups will take 3–5 minutes.)

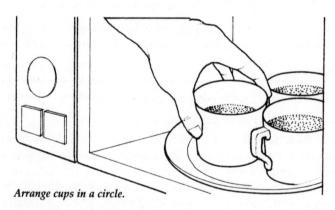

Arrange cups in a circle.

COMBINATION OVENS

Q *Exactly what is a combination oven?*

A A combination oven is usually a countertop oven about the size of a microwave cooker (although three full-size versions are available at the time of going to print). It combines several methods of cooking in one unit. These are usually microwave cooking, convection cooking and combination cooking. One model even has a ceramic hob on the top. These different methods of cooking can be used on their own or simultaneously.

C

Q *Please can you explain to me how the combination system works?*

A The combination system is a combination of cooking by convection and microwave energy, thus combining the advantages of both cooking methods; the browning and crisping effects of the convection system and the speed of microwave energy.

Q *How does the convection system work in a combination oven?*

A The convected heat can be supplied as ducted heat, ie. hot air forced into the cabinet, or as radiant heat from a top and bottom element. It is the top element in this design which functions as the grill.

Q *Is the microwave system in a combination oven the same as in a microwave cooker?*

A Yes, it is the same and, like microwave cookers, most combination ovens have several microwave settings although some have only DEFROST and HIGH settings. However, although the HIGH setting on most combination ovens is 600–650 watts, equivalent to the HIGH setting on most top-of-the-range microwave cookers on the market, food takes slightly longer to cook in a combination oven. This is probably due to design differences in the oven. You will need to bear this in mind if using recipes from a microwave cookery book.

Q *What are the advantages and disadvantages of a combination oven compared to a microwave cooker?*

A The advantages are that, unlike a microwave cooker, a combination oven browns and crisps food as well as cooking the food quickly. The disadvantages are that when used as a convection oven, the table-top combination oven is limited in size. The racks provided for two-tier cooking are only the diameter of the turntable and therefore considerably smaller than a conventional oven shelf. The oven can also be difficult to clean. (See **Cleaning**, page 39).

Auto Cook

Q *What is an auto cook device?*

A An auto cook device (called a sensor device on some models) is a more advanced and versatile version of the probe which is still available with some microwave cookers. Its operation varies from model to model. It works in one of two ways, either by being triggered when steam is released from food (humidity sensors) or by sensing the surface temperature of the food (infrared sensors).

Q *Do you think that an auto cook device is a useful feature to have on a combination oven?*

A This method of cooking works with a varying degree of success, depending on the type of food being cooked. It is really most useful if you can't be bothered to calculate cooking times for large pieces of meat or for convenience foods, but is not very helpful if you are trying to cook anything more adventurous.

Automatic Cooking

Q *How does automatic cooking work on a combination oven?*

A This feature, found on some models, is the same as an automatic cooking function on a conventional oven. You can programme the time you wish cooking to begin, the cooking temperature/power level and the cooking time.

Auto-Defrost

Q *What is an auto-defrost device and how does it work?*

A Auto-defrost is an automatic function offered on some combination ovens. It is controlled by the weight of the food. On some models, you programme in the weight of the food and the control calculates the defrosting time per 1 kg (2 lb). It may or may not include standing times. On more sophisticated models there is a crystal beneath the turntable which

monitors the deflection produced by the weight of food put on top of it and causes a voltage change which triggers the correct defrosting time.

Biscuits

Q *Would you recommend cooking biscuits in a combination oven?*

A No. The capacity of most combination ovens is less than a conventional oven (with the exception of a few full-size combination ovens on the market) and therefore space is limited for cooking batches of biscuits or small cakes. If you have the choice, you should therefore cook these in your full-size oven.

Cakes

Q *Can I bake a cake in my traditional metal tins when I cook on a combination setting?*

A No. Always use non-metal dishes rather than a metal cake tin, since metal reflects microwaves and makes it pointless cooking on combination. You can, of course, cook your favourite cake recipes in your ordinary metal cake tins on a convection setting. (See **Dishes** page 41 and **Insulating Mat** page 45 for more information.)

Q *Would you recommend cooking a cake in a preheated oven or is it not necessary?*

A I would recommend that you do preheat the oven when baking a cake as you tend to get a much browner result. Do this while you are preparing the cake mixture.

Q *My chocolate cake had patches of burnt sugar on the bottom. How can I avoid this happening next time?*

A Microwaves are particularly attracted to sugar and fat. Foods with a high sugar content should be watched very carefully during cooking to prevent burning. Make sure that you cream the cake mixture thoroughly to remove lumps of sugar and use a MEDIUM LOW or LOW setting.

Q *Can I speed up the cooking of my Christmas cake by cooking on combination?*

A No. Rich fruit cakes should be cooked on convection to achieve their moist texture and allow the flavours to develop.

Q *I made my favourite cake recipe and cooked it on a combination setting. It rose very quickly and looked cooked, but when I turned it out it was raw in the middle. What went wrong?*

A The temperature and microwave setting were too high. Reduce the setting next time. Alternatively, the recipe may not be suitable or the dish-size incorrect. Try using a larger dish or a ring mould.

Q *I baked a cake on combination; it was cooked but did not go brown. How can I ensure a golden brown crust on my cakes?*

A Check your microwave setting. If it is too high the microwaves will cook the cake before it has a chance to brown. Always preheat the oven before cooking cakes.

Q *I made some small cakes and cooked them on combination but they did not brown. What should I do next time to ensure they do?*

A Small items such as cakes and biscuits are best cooked on convection because on combination the cooking time is so short they do not have time to brown or form a crust.

Casseroles and Stews

Q *Can you give me some hints for cooking meat casseroles successfully in the combination oven?*

A • Use the oven to its full potential by using the microwave setting to soften vegetables or to make a sauce before cooking the casserole on a combination setting.

• When cooking casseroles, cover them tightly with a heavy plate or lid to prevent the liquid evaporating.

• Stir frequently for even cooking.

Cleaning

Q *What is the best way to clean a combination oven?*

A Microwave cooking does not make much mess in the oven interior, since there is no dry heat to stick the food to the sides of the oven or to bake it on. However, with combination cooking the oven will get just as dirty as in conventional cooking. Unlike conventional ovens, the interior must not be cleaned with abrasive materials as this will damage the metal lining. It is best to wipe the oven after each use with a soft cloth dipped in soapy water. For more stubborn dirt, foam and liquid cleaners can be used, but should not be applied directly to the oven interior; put them on a cloth first. To remove stubborn grease splashes left after roasting it is helpful to steam them off first. To soften some of the baked-on food, fill a large bowl with water and microwave on HIGH for 5 minutes or until rapidly boiling. Then wipe the food off with a cloth. Turntables, racks and splash trivets can all be removed from the oven and soaked in soapy water. Easy-clean oven linings are available on some models.

Q *I have heard of combination ovens with Pyrolytic cleaning. What is this?*

A Pyrolytic cleaning removes soiling left on the sides of ovens without the need for elbow grease. In this system the oven door is locked automatically and a very high temperature set for a specified time. All soiling is burned off and can be brushed out when the oven is cool.

Cookery Books

Q *I would like to buy a combination oven cookery book. Is there one in particular that you would recommend?*

A Yes! My colleagues, Janet Smith and Emma-Lee Gow, have written the *Good Housekeeping Combination Oven Cookbook*. It contains 150 delicious recipes, all of which are compatible with every type of combination oven. The recipes have been double tested in the Good Housekeeping kitchens, and

helpful information with each recipe ensures success every time.

Cooking

Q *How do you cook on combination?*

A To cook on combination (also known as 'Hi-speed' or 'dual cook'), you must first set the temperature in °C for the convection system and then set the microwave level. Some books and manufacturers generally recommend cooking on a HIGH microwave setting and at 250°C. This certainly cooks the food quickly but the food tends to dry out and often burns on the outside. A better combination of settings to use is 200°C/MEDIUM LOW. On some ovens, the combination setting is preset. This means that you can change the temperature but not the microwave output, making it harder to cook some foods on combination. Achieving the correct combination of convected heat and microwave energy is very important and can be quite difficult to understand, so read the introduction to combination ovens on page 9 before cooking on combination.

Q *How do you cook on convection?*

A If you select this method of cooking (also known as 'turbo' or 'conventional heat'), it is the same as cooking in an ordinary electric oven. The convection system in most combination ovens is fan-assisted, that is the hot air is circulated in the oven by a fan. This has the effect of speeding up the cooking process, so if you are cooking recipes designed for cooking in an ordinary oven, you will need to reduce the temperature by 10°C.

Q *Which cooking methods do you recommend for which types of foods?*

A Use the combination setting for roasts, pies, pastry, casseroles, baked potatoes, pot roasts and baked chops. Use the convection setting for roasting small game birds, fruit cakes, meringues, choux pastry, biscuits, small cakes and buns.

Use the microwave setting for moist methods of cooking, such as poaching, or whenever you don't expect a brown appearance. It is good for vegetables, fish, soups, pasta, rice and sauces, as well as for thawing and reheating.

Cooking Techniques

Q *Are there special cooking techniques for combination ovens?*

A Yes. If you are familiar with microwave cookery, you will understand the importance of certain cooking techniques such as arranging, covering, turning, stirring, pricking and slashing food. If you are new to this method of cooking, read the microwave chapter first.

Dishes

Q *What dishes should I use in a combination oven? I've heard that some say not to use metal dishes.*

A There is a great deal of confusion about this. Some manufacturers say that metal can be used when cooking on combination (with the insulating mat in position) while others say it must be avoided. To prevent any errors, it is best to use ovenproof glass and ceramics for all methods of cooking except convection. There is also a range of microware available which can be used up to 200°C. When cooking on convection only, use any of your usual metal baking tins. For combination and microwave cooking, stick to ovenproof plastics, ceramics and glass.

Fish

Q *Which is the best method for cooking fish in a combination oven?*

A Fish may be cooked by microwave, combination or in the usual way, by convection. Fish cooks quickly and easily on the microwave setting and the results are similar to those obtained when it is conventionally steamed or poached. The combination setting also cooks fish quickly but gives

whole fish a crisper skin. It also allows you to widen your repertoire and cook crisp-topped gratins and pies.

Q *How long does fish take to cook in the combination oven?*

A Follow the chart below. If cooking on microwave only, place the fish in a large shallow dish with 30 ml (2 tbsp) stock, wine, milk or water per 450 g (1 lb) fish (unless otherwise stated), then cover and cook as shown in the chart. Alternatively, cook whole fish on a combination setting. Place the fish in a large shallow dish, slash the skin and brush with butter. This chart is only a guide. Always check before the end of the calculated cooking time to prevent overcooking.

Type	Time/Setting	Notes
Whole round fish (whiting, mullet, trout, carp, bream, small haddock)	4 minutes on microwave HIGH per 450 g (1 lb) or 6–8 minutes per 450 g (1 lb) on combination at 200°C/MEDIUM LOW	Slash skin to prevent bursting. Turn fish over halfway through cooking time if fish weighs more than 1.4 kg (3 lb). Reposition fish if cooking more than two.
Whole flat fish (plaice, sole)	3 minutes on microwave HIGH per 450 g (1 lb) or 4–5 minutes per 450 g (1 lb) on combination at 200°C/MEDIUM LOW	Slash skin. Check fish after 2 minutes.
Cutlets, steaks, thick fish fillets (cod, coley, haddock, halibut, monkfish fillet)	4 minutes on microwave HIGH per 450 g (1 lb) or 5–6 minutes per 450 g (1 lb) on combination at 200°C/MEDIUM LOW	Position thicker parts towards the outside of the dish. Turn halfway through cooking if steaks are very thick.
Flat fish fillets (plaice, sole)	2–3 minutes on microwave HIGH per 450 g (1 lb)	Check fish after 2 minutes.
Dense fish fillets, cutlets, steaks (tuna, swordfish, conger eel), whole monkfish tail	5–6 minutes on microwave HIGH per 450 g (1 lb) or 7–8 minutes per 450 g (1 lb) on combination at 200°C/MEDIUM LOW	Position thicker parts towards the outside of the dish. Turn halfway through cooking if steaks are thick.

Fish Cooking Times ... contd.

Type	Time/Setting	Notes
Skate wings	6–7 minutes on microwave HIGH per 450 g (1 lb)	Add 150 ml (¼ pint) stock or milk. If cooking more than 900 g (2 lb) cook in batches.
Smoked fish	Cook as appropriate for type of fish, e.g. whole, fillet or cutlet. See above	
Squid	Put prepared squid, cut into rings, in a large bowl with 150 ml (¼ pint) wine, stock or water per 450 g (1 lb). Cook, covered, on microwave HIGH for 5–8 minutes per 450 g (1 lb)	Time depends on size of squid – larger, older, squid are tougher and may take longer to cook.
Octopus	Put prepared octopus, cut into 2.5 cm (1 inch) pieces, in a large bowl with 150 ml (¼ pint) wine, stock or water per 450 g (1 lb). Cook, covered, on microwave HIGH until liquid is boiling, then on MEDIUM for 15–20 minutes per 450 g (1 lb)	Tenderise octopus before cooking by beating vigorously with a meat mallet or rolling pin. Marinate before cooking to help tenderise. Time depends on age and size of octopus.
Scallops (shelled)	2–4 minutes on microwave HIGH per 450 g (1 lb)	Do not overcook or scallops will be tough. Add corals for 1–2 minutes at end of cooking time.
Scallops in their shells	Do not cook in the combination oven	Cook conventionally
Mussels	Put up to 900 g (2 lb) mussels in a large bowl with 150 ml (¼ pint) wine, stock or water. Cook, covered, on microwave HIGH for 3–5 minutes	Remove mussels on the top as they cook. Shake the bowl occasionally during cooking. Discard any mussels which do not open.

Fish Cooking Times . . . contd.

Type	Time/Setting	Notes
Cockles	Put cockles in a large bowl with a little water. Cook, covered, on microwave HIGH for 3–4 minutes until the shells open. Take cockles out of their shells and cook for a further 2–3 minutes or until hot	Shake the bowl occasionally during cooking.
Raw prawns	2–5 minutes on microwave HIGH per 450 g (1 lb), stirring frequently	Time depends on the size of the prawns. Cook until their colour changes to bright pink.
Live crab or lobster	Do not cook in the combination oven	Cook conventionally.
Small clams	Cook as mussels	As mussels.
Large clams	Do not cook in the combination oven	Cook conventionally.

Foil

Q *Can I use foil in my combination oven?*

A No. Foil should not be used on either the microwave or the combination setting. However, it is quite safe to use when cooking on convection only. (See FOIL, page 73 for further information.)

Grill

Q *Do you consider it necessary to buy a combination oven with a grill?*

A Whether you choose a combination oven with a grill depends on the other cooking appliances that you already have. In combination ovens in which the convected heat is supplied by radiant heat from an element, it is this element which functions as the grill.

C

Halogen Heat

Q *I have seen a combination oven that cooks by halogen heat. What is this?*

A Some combination ovens use halogen heat as an alternative to the convection method. Heat is created by halogen gas-filled bulbs in the top and sides of the oven. These emit heat and light.

Insulating Mat

Q *What is an insulating mat used for?*

A This piece of equipment is supplied with some ovens while others suggest using an ovenproof plate instead. It should be put on the wire rack when cooking something in a metal baking tin on combination and its use is to prevent the two metal surfaces from coming into contact with each other, thus preventing sparking. However, since microwave energy cannot pass through metal, it seems pointless to use metal containers on a combination setting and its use is therefore unnecessary.

Meat

Q *I cooked a joint of meat on combination; it was very brown on the outside but still raw in the middle. What went wrong?*

A The cooking temperature was too high. When roasting meat it is best cooked on combination at 200°C/MEDIUM LOW.

Q *When roasting meat on combination the fat splashes a lot, making a mess of the oven. How can I stop this?*

A Meat will always splash during cooking and, because the capacity of the oven is much smaller than a conventional oven, it is concentrated on a smaller area and seems worse. Draining off excess fat halfway through cooking, placing the meat in a shallow dish rather than directly on the wire rack, and reducing the microwave setting all help to reduce splashing.

Q *I roasted a leg of lamb on combination and it seemed cooked, but when we came to eat it, it was very tough. Why was this?*

A The lamb was overcooked. See **Roasting** on page 48 and refer to the chart for cooking times. Also, the microwave setting may have been too high.

Q *I followed my favourite casserole recipe but when it was cooked the liquid had evaporated. How can I prevent this happening?*

A Always check casseroles and stir frequently during cooking. Cover tightly with a heavy lid or ovenproof plate. Add extra liquid if necessary.

Memory

Q *What is a memory device?*

A This device, found on some models, can store several sets of cooking instructions – useful if you often cook the same dish.

Multiple Sequence Cooking

Q *What is multiple sequence cooking?*

A This function, found on some ovens, enables you to pro- gramme in a series of power settings and times in advance if you are cooking a dish requiring more than one setting.

Oven Temperature

Q *The heat controls on my combination oven are Celsius but I usually cook in Fahrenheit; what temperature should I select?*

A The heat controls on all combination ovens are given in Celsius, so follow the chart opposite if you usually cook in Fahrenheit or by gas. You will notice that these are not the exact conversions because the °C have been reduced by 10°C to allow for the speed of cooking in a combination oven. The temperature range on most combination ovens is 40–350°C, but if your oven has a limited range choose the temperature nearest the one you need and adjust the cooking time.

C

OVEN TEMPERATURE SCALES

° Celsius Scale	Electric Scale °F	Gas Oven Marks
100	225	¼
120	250	½
130	275	1
140	300	2
160	325	3
170	350	4
180	375	5
190	400	6
200	425	7
220	450	8
230	475	9

Pastry

Q *The puff pastry on my pie rose very quickly and unevenly and lost its shape during cooking on combination. How can I prevent it from rising so much?*

A Puff pastry rises very well on a combination setting so roll it out a little more thinly than usual.

Poultry and Game

Q *How long does it take to cook the various types of poultry in a combination oven?*

A Follow the chart below for the cooking times.

Poultry roasting times per 450 g (1 lb) on combination at 220°C/MEDIUM LOW

Type		Time
Chicken	Whole	8–10 minutes
	Quarters	8–10 minutes
	Drumsticks	10–12 minutes
Turkey	Whole	6–8 minutes
Duck	Whole	8–10 minutes finish cooking on convection at 250°C for 5 minutes if skin is not crisp enough
	Quarters	8–10 minutes
Goose	Whole	9–11 minutes

C
COMBINATION OVENS

Q *What is the best way to cook whole game birds?*

A Game birds are best cooked on convection only as they tend to become dry if cooked on combination. Follow a recipe in a conventional cook book for the oven temperature, remembering to reduce the usual oven setting by 10°C to allow for the fast-cooking, fan-assisted system. Cook for the usual time.

Preheating

Q *Do you recommend preheating the oven before cooking?*

A Small items, such as chops, chicken portions, small pastries, cakes and pies, for example, benefit from going straight into a hot oven. They cook very quickly by microwave energy because they are small, and so do not stay in the oven long enough to be browned by the convected heat. Always preheat on convection only. Ten minutes is usually long enough for most ovens, but check your manufacturer's handbook first.

Reheating

Q *What is the best way to reheat food in the combination oven?*

A Most foods are best reheated on a HIGH microwave setting. One of the advantages of a combination oven is that it is ideal for heating the foods that don't reheat well on microwave alone. Reheated pies, pastries and bread are no longer soggy but retain their crisp texture. Reheat at a temperature of 200–250°C combined with a MEDIUM LOW microwave setting.

Roasting

Q *Can you give me some hints for roasting meat successfully?*

A • If your oven comes with a splash trivet and wire rack, then you can roast meat standing on the rack, with a splash trivet in position below, on the turntable. (Roast

potatoes can then be cooked on the splash trivet.) Alternatively, place the joint in a large, shallow dish and stand the dish on the wire rack. This second method is often preferred since it reduces splashing and it is simpler and safer to handle the meat in the dish rather than placing it directly on the rack.

- Small joints of meat weighing less than 1.1 kg (2½ lb), other than rack of lamb, are best cooked on convection only.

- It is not necessary to preheat the oven when cooking large joints, but when cooking chops, or other small items with a short cooking time, the results are better if the oven is preheated.

- Turning the joint halfway through cooking is sometimes recommended, but it is really not necessary.

Q *Can you tell me how long to roast the various types of meat in a combination oven?*

A The following chart will help you.

Meat roasting times per 450 g (1 lb) on combination at 200°C/MEDIUM LOW

Type		Time
Lamb		
	Leg	medium: 10–12 minutes
		well done: 12–14 minutes
	Rack of lamb	medium: 10–12 minutes
	Chops	10–12 minutes
Beef		
	Rib or topside	rare: 8–10 minutes
		medium: 10–12 minutes
		well done: 12–14 minutes
Pork		
	Leg, Loin or Shoulder	15–18 minutes
	Chops	11–12 minutes

Splash Trivet

Q *What is a splash trivet for?*

A The purpose of a splash trivet is to shield the cooking liquid or fat from microwave energy, preventing it from splashing and absorbing energy needed to cook the food.

Q *How and when do you use a splash trivet?*

A The splash trivet is put directly on top of the turntable, under the wire rack, when cooking roasts or anything else likely to produce a lot of fat or juice during cooking. The liquid drips through the wire rack and the splash trivet on to the turntable. Most oven manufacturers recommend the use of the splash trivet with the wire rack and turntable, but it is rather awkward to use and preferable to cook a roast standing in a large shallow dish on the wire rack. However, it is not possible to cook very large joints or a turkey in a dish, so use the splash trivet for these.

Thawing

Q *How do I use a combination oven for thawing foods?*

A Thawing should always be done on a low microwave setting. Alternatively, some ovens have an auto-defrost function (see page 36).

Wire Rack

Q *What is the purpose of the wire rack, supplied with my combination oven?*

A The wire rack is rather like a roasting rack. It stands on the turntable during cooking. Its purpose is to raise the food in the oven, thereby helping it to brown more quickly (rather like putting food on the top shelf in a conventional oven). Some combination ovens come with two wire racks, thus creating two shelves for two-level cooking.

Q *My oven does not have a wire rack with it; should it have one?*

A If your oven does not have a wire rack it will have a slide-out shelf instead, which does the same job.

Q *Do you recommend using the wire rack for cooking?*

A Yes. It is best to leave the lowest wire rack or shelf in position on the turntable for all modes of cooking. However, if you are cooking something in a large, deep dish, or a large joint that will not fit on the rack in the oven, you can achieve satisfactory results without it.

Q *I thought you shouldn't put metal in the oven when cooking on the microwave setting, but the wire rack in my combination oven is made of metal; is it safe?*

A Yes, it is safe to use it when cooking on the microwave setting because the pattern of microwaves is designed to go between the wire supports.

COOKER SETTINGS

Q *The recipes in my cookery books are written for a 600-watt cooker but I have a 500-watt cooker. Can you tell me how much extra cooking and thawing time I should allow?*

A Add approximately 10–15 seconds per minute for a 500-watt cooker, and 15–20 seconds per minute for a 400-watt cooker. No matter what the wattage of your cooker is, you should always check food before the end of cooking time to ensure that it does not get overcooked. Don't forget, also, to allow for standing time.

Q *Some of the recipes in my cookery books tell me to cook on a* HIGH *setting but the settings on my cooker are from 1 to 9, so how do I calculate which setting to use?*

A Whatever the wattage of your cooker, the HIGH/FULL setting will always be 100% of the cooker's output. Thus your highest setting will correspond to HIGH. To work out the

equivalents of MEDIUM and LOW, use the following calculation.

MEDIUM (60%) = %
power required × total
number of cooker
settings ÷ 100

$$\text{e.g.} = \frac{60 \times 9}{100} = 5$$

LOW (35%) = %
power required × total
number of cooker
settings ÷ 100

$$\text{e.g.} = \frac{35 \times 9}{100} = 3$$

COOKING

Q *What foods can't I cook in the microwave?*

A The following foods can't be cooked in the microwave:

- Boiled eggs (they explode)
- Deep and shallow fried foods (it isn't possible to control the temperature of the oil)
- Yorkshire pudding, choux pastry, soufflés and conventional meringue mixture (they don't rise)
- Roast potatoes and parsnips (they don't brown)
- Stews and casseroles using ingredients needing long, slow cooking (the meat won't become tender)
- Large, rich fruit cakes (they need long, slow cooking)
- Foods with a batter coating (the batter will not become crisp)
- Large turkeys (the cooker cavity is not large enough)
- Puddings containing alcohol (they reach too high a temperature and can easily burn)

Q *Does food in the microwave cook from the outside in or from the inside out? I've heard different opinions.*

A Contrary to the once-held belief that microwaves cook from the inside out, the outer edges of food cook first in the microwave. This is because microwaves only penetrate food to a depth of about 5 cm (2 inches). After that, the food cooks towards the centre by the conduction of heat.

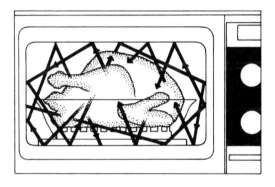

Food cooks towards the centre by the conduction of heat.

Q *I always seem to overcook food in the microwave so that it becomes dry. What should I do?*

A Undercook all food! Overcooked food will be dry and this cannot be rectified whereas undercooked dishes can always be returned to the microwave for further cooking.

Q *Can I cook several dishes of food at once in the microwave?*

A This is not advisable because when you increase the volume of food in the microwave, you must also increase the cooking time and therefore the value of cooking food at speed is wasted.

Q *Is it possible to cook an entire meal in the microwave?*

A This is possible but, since only one dish at a time should be cooked in the microwave, careful planning will be required as regards selecting the menu and cooking the food in the right sequence.

Q *I often find that parts of a dish are cooked, and others not. How can I ensure that food cooks evenly?*

A The following hints will help you.

- Make sure that the foods you are cooking are all cut to the same size.

- Since the outer edges of food normally cook first in the microwave, whenever possible, stir several times during cooking, from the outside of the dish towards the centre, to produce an evenly cooked result

- Foods such as meatballs, that cannot be stirred, should be rearranged during cooking. Move food from the outside of the dish towards the centre, and any in the centre to the outside of the dish.

- Single items thicker than 6 cm (2½ inches) will cook more evenly if they are turned over once during cooking, because the microwave signal is stronger towards the upper part of the cooker. This is particularly important when the food is not covered. When turning food over, reposition so that the outside parts are placed in the centre of the dish.

- Foods that cannot be stirred, because it would spoil the arrangement, and foods like large cakes, which cannot be repositioned or turned over, can be evenly cooked by rotating the dish once or twice during the cooking time. This is usually necessary even when the cooker has a turntable. It is particularly important if you find that cakes rise unevenly or if your cooker has hot or cold spots.

- When cooking several whole items of food, arrange them in a circle or square to ensure even cooking. Do not put anything in the centre as the microwaves penetrate the outside foods first.

COOKING TIME

Q *Do some foods cook more quickly than others in the microwave?*

A Yes. Foods which are high in fat or sugar will cook or reheat more quickly than those which are low in these ingredients, and food with a high moisture content will take longer to cook or reheat than drier foods.

Q *I find that cooking times vary quite a lot even though I am cooking the same quantity of a particular food each time. Is this possible?*

A Yes. This is possible because apart from the quantity of food, various other factors affect cooking times, such as whether the ingredients are warm or cold, whether you have just used the cooker and the floor is still warm and the type of cookware used.

COVERING

Q *When should I cover food, and when should I not?*

A Food should be covered to prevent drying out, therefore cover foods such as soups, fish, vegetables and fruit to retain the moisture. Do not cover dry foods such as pastries or those which require constant attention such as sauces and scrambled eggs.

Q *What should I use to cover food when cooking in the microwave?*

A A plate, lid, roasting bag or absorbent kitchen paper will all be suitable for covering food in the microwave. Roasting bags should be pierced or slit to allow the build-up of steam to escape during cooking, and should be tied with non-metallic ties.

The use of cling film should be avoided in microwave

cooking, as it has been found that the di-ez-ethyhexledipate (DEHA) used to soften cling film can migrate into the food during cooking. Foil should also not be used during cooking as it can easily cause ARCING though it is useful for wrapping meat during STANDING TIME.

Q *I have read, though, that there is a cling film that is safe to use, so can't I use that instead?*

A You can, but it doesn't cling when used for cooking! I therefore think it is worth being prudent and a plate or lid really is the best cover to use when you would otherwise use cling film.

Open the lid away from you.

CREME CARAMEL

Q *How do I cook crème caramel in the microwave without it curdling?*

A Here is a foolproof recipe. You must follow the recipe and method exactly for perfect results. It will serve 4.

Caramel
45 ml (3 level tbsp) caster sugar
25 ml (5 tsp) water

Crème
300 ml (½ pint) chilled milk
30 ml (2 level tbsp) caster sugar
5 ml (1 level tsp) cornflour
1.25 ml (¼ tsp) vanilla flavouring
2 eggs, size 2

1   To make the caramel, put the sugar and water in a 600 ml (1 pint) soufflé dish and cook on HIGH for 1½ minutes. Stir until the sugar dissolves then cook on HIGH for 3–4 minutes until the sugar is golden brown.
2   Holding the dish with oven gloves, tilt to coat the sides with caramel.
3   To make the crème, put everything except the eggs in a jug and cook on HIGH for 2 minutes or until nearly boiling. Stir, then whisk in the eggs.
4   Strain into the soufflé dish, cover and cook on LOW for 4–4½ minutes, turning the dish three times, until just set. Leave until cold. To serve, invert on to a serving dish.

CROISSANTS

Q   *Can I warm croissants in the microwave?*

A   Only if you like them soggy! Croissants contain a lot of fat, which attract microwave energy, and because of this they collapse and become soggy when cooked in a microwave. If overcooked they become hard. For the best possible result, wrap loosely in kitchen paper or a napkin and cook on HIGH. Two croissants will take about 30 seconds.

CROUTONS

Q   *Can I make croûtons in a microwave?*

A   Yes. To make them, remove the crusts from a slice of bread and spread both sides generously with butter. Sprinkle with paprika and cut into 1 cm (½ inch) cubes. Arrange in a circle on a sheet of greaseproof paper and cook on HIGH for 1–2 minutes until firm; turning once.

CUSTARD

Q *Can I make custard in the microwave and if so, how do I make it?*

A The answer is yes and it is made in the same way as a savoury white sauce. Here is the recipe.

30 ml (2 level tbsp) custard powder or 600 ml (1 pint) packet
15–30 ml (1–2 level tbsp) sugar
568 ml (1 pint) milk

1 Blend the custard powder and sugar with a little of the milk in a medium bowl. Stir in the remaining milk.

2 Cook on HIGH for 3–4 minutes or until the sauce has thickened, stirring every minute. Stir well and serve hot or cold.

See also EGG CUSTARD, page 63.

D

DENSITY

Q *Does the density of a food affect its cooking time in the microwave?*

A Yes. A dense food such as meat will take longer to cook, reheat or thaw than porous, light and airy foods such as bread, cakes and puddings. This is because microwaves cannot penetrate as deeply into denser, heavier foods.

DISHES

Q *Do I have to buy special dishes for cooking in the microwave?*

A No. You will find that much of your standard cookware is suitable for microwave use, provided it isn't metal. Do not use items which are decorated with gold or silver or products that contain metal particles. Materials like

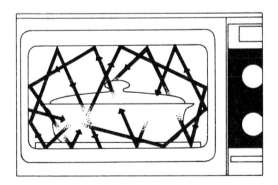

Microwaves are transmitted through materials.

D

DISHES

ovenproof glass, ceramic glass and china work well in the microwave cooker, however, as they allow the microwave energy to pass through them to the food. Although microwaves will not be absorbed by the cooking dish, it may become hot during cooking because heat is conducted from the food to the container. This can happen either during long periods of cooking or when using foods containing a high proportion of sugar or fat. For this reason, less durable containers, such as those made of soft plastics, paper or wicker, should only be used for brief cooking times. (See below for dishes that cannot be used.)

Q *What dishes shouldn't I use in the microwave?*

A Metal reflects microwaves, so should not be used for cooking in the microwave. Also avoid using china or glass decorated with metal paint. Metal produces arcing which can damage the cooker's magnetron.

Q *Does it matter what size dish I use in the microwave?*

A Yes. The depth of the dish, for example, is important. Foods cooked in shallow dishes cook more quickly than those in deep dishes. Choose cooking dishes that are large enough to hold the quantity of food and avoid overfilling – this not only results in spillages but also prevents even cooking. Dishes should be large enough to hold foods such as fish, chicken joints or chops in a single layer.

Q *Does the shape of the dish matter?*

A The shape of your cookware is important because of the patterns in which the microwaves move around the cooker cavity. Round containers are preferable to square ones, for example, as they have no corners in which clusters of microwaves can concentrate, overcooking the food at these points. Straight-sided containers are more efficient than sloping ones, which cause food at the shallower outer edge to cook more quickly. A ring-shaped container will always give the best results of all as the micro-wave energy can enter from both sides as well as the top, giving more even cooking.

DRIED FRUIT

Q *Can I use the microwave to plump up dried fruit?*

A Yes. Put the dried fruit in a bowl, cover with water, milkless tea or fruit juice and cook on HIGH for 5 minutes. Stir, leave to stand for 5 minutes then drain well.

Q *In my favourite fruit cake recipe, the dried fruit is left to soak overnight in fruit juice. Can the microwave help me save time?*

A Yes, overnight soaking plumps the fruit. To save time, put the fruit and fruit juice in a heatproof bowl, cover and cook on HIGH for 2–5 minutes (depending on the quantity). Stir the fruit thoroughly and if it is still cold cook for a further 2 minutes or until just warm. Leave until cold then proceed with your recipe as normal.

DYEING

Q *I've heard that it is possible to dye fabrics in the microwave. Is this true and if so how do you do it?*

A Yes. But it is only possible to dye up to 225 g (8 oz) of fabric at one time. Fabrics made from natural fibres may be dyed this way but wool and synthetic fabrics are unsuitable. Clothes with metal such as zips can obviously not be dyed. To micro-dye, wash the fabric and leave damp. Wearing rubber gloves tip one pack (100 g/4 oz) Dylon natural fabric dye into a large bowl. Gradually add 200 ml (7 fl oz) cold water and stir with a plastic spatula, until the dye is dissolved. Add 400 ml (14 fl oz) cold water. Immerse the fabric in the dye solution. Put the bowl in a plastic bag in the microwave and cook on HIGH for 4 minutes. Remove the bowl from the cooker and tip away the dye solution. Rinse the fabric in cold water until that water is running almost clear. Finally, wash the fabric in hot water and washing powder and dry away from direct heat or sunlight. Patterned effects such as tie-dye can be created by knotting and twisting. (See Dylon's micro-dye leaflets for instructions.)

DUMPLINGS

Q *Can I cook dumplings in a microwave?*

A Yes. They cook well. Make up the suet pastry to a conventional recipe and form into small balls. Add the dumplings to a hot casserole, arranging them around the edge of the bowl or dish. Cover and cook on HIGH for a further 5 minutes or until the dumplings have risen.

E

EGG CUSTARD

Q *Is it possible to cook an egg custard in the microwave?*

A Yes, but sauces thickened with egg are best cooked on a LOW setting to prevent them curdling. Here is the recipe for the classic custard sauce.

300 ml (½ pint) milk
2 eggs
15 ml (1 level tbsp) granulated sugar
few drops of vanilla flavouring

1 Pour the milk into a large measuring jug and cook on HIGH for 2 minutes or until hot.

2 Lightly whisk the eggs, sugar and vanilla flavouring together in a bowl. Add the heated milk and mix well.

3 Cook on high for 1 minute, then cook on LOW for 4½ minutes or until the custard thinly coats the back of a spoon. Whisk several times during cooking. This sauce thickens slightly on cooling. Serve hot or cold.

See also CUSTARD, page 58 and CREME CARAMEL, page 56.

EGGS

Q *Can I boil an egg in the microwave?*

A No. Pressure builds up and it will explode.

Q *Can I poach eggs in the microwave?*

A Yes. But it is not necessary to use water, as in a conventional

Prick the egg yolk before cooking.

recipe. The following recipe is the microwave equivalent.

2–4 eggs

1 Break 2–4 eggs into ramekin dishes or teacups. Gently prick the yolks with a fine skewer or the tip of a sharp knife. Arrange the dishes in a circle in the cooker. Cook on HIGH until the egg whites are just set. (Two eggs will take 45 seconds to 1 minute, four eggs will take 1½–2 minutes.) Leave to stand for 2 minutes.

Q *How do I stop eggs, once broken, from bursting and exploding all over the microwave when I cook them?*

A It is very important to prick the egg yolks with a fine skewer or the tip of a sharp knife so that they do not burst, but even then you must watch and listen for popping. If they do pop, quickly move their position in the cooker.

Q *When I cook scrambled eggs in the microwave they always go too hard. Where am I going wrong, and what can I do for perfect results?*

A The reason they are hard is because you are overcooking them. For perfect results, follow the recipe opposite.

SCRAMBLED EGGS

SERVES 2

4 eggs
60 ml (4 tbsp) milk
25 g (1 oz) butter or margarine
salt and pepper

1   Put all the ingredients in a medium bowl and whisk together.

2   Cook on HIGH for 1½ minutes until the mixture just begins to set around the edge of the bowl. Whisk well to incorporate the set egg mixture.

3   Cook on HIGH for a further 1½–2 minutes, whisking every 30 seconds until the eggs are just set but still very soft.

Whisk scrambled eggs during cooking.

EN PAPILLOTE

Q *Can I cook en papillote in a microwave cooker?*

A Yes. This simple method of cooking fish in greaseproof paper parcels works well in the microwave. Here is a recipe for you to try.

Fish en Papillote

Serves 2

2 small fish such as red mullet, each weighing about 175 g (6 oz)
  cleaned and scaled
salt and pepper
½ small onion, skinned and thinly sliced
2 parsley sprigs
2 bay leaves
2 slices of lemon

1 Slash the fish on each side using a sharp knife. Season the insides with salt and pepper to taste. Use the onion, parsley sprigs, bay leaves and lemon slices to stuff the fish.

2 Cut two 30.5 cm (12 inch) squares of greaseproof paper. Place a fish on each piece and fold it to make a neat parcel, twisting the ends together to seal. Place on a large flat plate.

3 Cook on HIGH for 3–4 minutes or until the fish is tender. Serve the fish in their parcels.

F

FAT

Q *I am trying to cut down the amount of fat I eat. Is microwave cooking a good method for a low-fat diet?*

A Yes. It is excellent, because as the food doesn't stick to the dish, there being no direct heat, you can cut down and sometimes eliminate the amount of fat normally used. Baked aubergines for moussaka (see page 134) and scrambled eggs (see page 65) are both good examples.

FISH AND SHELLFISH

Q *Can I thaw frozen fish in its original wrapper?*

A Yes, but remember to slash the wrappings first.

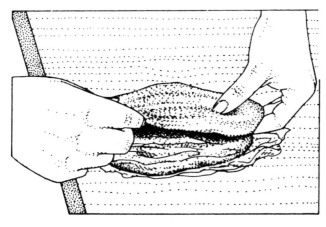

Separating frozen fish fillets.

F

FISH AND SHELLFISH

Q *How long should I allow to thaw fish in the microwave?*

A Follow the chart below. Separate cutlets, fillets or steaks as soon as possible during thawing, and remove pieces from the cooker as soon as they are thawed. Timing will depend on the thickness of the fish.

Type	Time/Setting	Notes
Whole round fish (mullet, trout, carp, bream, whiting)	4–6 minutes per 450 g (1 lb) on LOW or DEFROST	*Stand* for 5 minutes after each 2–3 minutes. Very large fish are thawed more successfully if left to stand for 10–15 minutes after every 2–3 minutes.
White fish fillets or cutlets (cod, haddock, halibut, monkfish), whole plaice or sole	3–4 minutes per 450 g (1 lb) on LOW or DEFROST	*Stand* for 5 minutes after each 2–3 minutes.
Lobster, crab, crab claws	6–8 minutes per 450 g (1 lb) on LOW or DEFROST	*Stand* for 5 minutes after each 2–3 minutes.
Crab meat	4–6 minutes per 450 g (1 lb) block on LOW or DEFROST	*Stand* for 5 minutes after each 2–3 minutes.
Prawns, shrimps, scampi, scallops	2–3 minutes per 100 g (4 oz) 3–4 minutes per 225 g (8 oz) on LOW or DEFROST	*Arrange* in a circle on a double sheet of absorbent kitchen paper to absorb liquid. Separate during thawing with a fork and remove pieces from cooker as they thaw.

Q *Can you give me some hints for cooking fish successfully in the microwave?*

A • When cooking whole fish, slash their skins in two or three places on both sides to prevent them bursting during cooking.

  • Arrange small whole fish in a cartwheel, the tails towards the centre, for more even cooking.

F

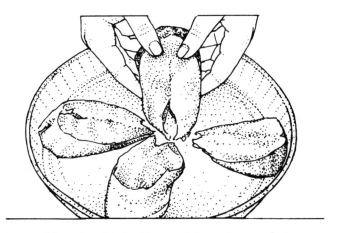

Arrange fish steaks with the thinner ends facing in towards the centre.

- When cooking fish steaks, arrange them with the thinner ends facing in towards the centre of the container.

- Large fish should be cooked in a single layer and turned over once during cooking.

- Season fish with salt after cooking to prevent it toughening and drying out the flesh.

- To prevent fish drying out, brush skin with melted butter or margarine.

- Remember that fish cooks very quickly so take care not to let it overcook. Shellfish is particularly critical. Take into account the standing time, as during this time the heat will equalise throughout the food.

- Fillets of fish may be cooked flat or rolled up. Reposition during cooking.

- When cooking fish fillets flat, overlap thin parts to prevent overcooking of the thinner ends.

F

- Boil-in-the-bag fish such as kippers can be cooked in their bags. Pierce the bag before cooking.

- Fish in batter which has been fried conventionally will not reheat well as the batter goes soggy.

- Fish is cooked when the flesh flakes easily and is opaque. Overcooking fish will toughen the flesh.

- Unless instructions are given to the contrary, always cover fish when cooking.

Q *Can you tell me how and how long to cook the various types of fish in the microwave?*

A Simply put the fish in a single layer in a shallow dish with 30 ml (2 tbsp) stock, wine, milk or water per 450 g (1 lb) of fish (unless otherwise stated), then cover and cook as below. The cooking time depends on the thickness of the fish as well as the amount being cooked and whether it is cooked whole, in fillets or cut up into smaller pieces. This chart is a guide only. Always check before the end of the calculated cooking time to prevent overcooking.

Type	Time/Setting	Microwave Cooking Technique(s)
Whole round fish (whiting, mullet, trout, carp, bream, small haddock)	4 minutes on HIGH per 450 g (1 lb)	*Slash* skin to prevent bursting. *Turn* fish over halfway through cooking time if fish weighs more than 1.4 kg (3 lb). *Reposition* fish if cooking more than two.
Whole flat fish (plaice, sole)	3 minutes on HIGH per 450 g (1 lb)	*Slash* skin. Check fish after 2 minutes.
Cutlets, steaks, thick fish fillets (cod, coley, haddock, halibut, monkfish fillet)	4 minutes on HIGH per 450 g (1 lb)	*Position* thicker parts towards the outside of the dish. *Turn* halfway through cooking if steaks are very thick.

Fish Cooking Chart ... contd.

Type	Time/Setting	Microwave Cooking Technique(s)
Flat fish fillets (plaice, sole)	2–3 minutes on HIGH per 450 g (1 lb)	*Check* fish after 2 minutes.
Dense fish fillets, cutlets, steaks (tuna, swordfish, conger eel), whole monkfish tail	5–6 minutes on HIGH per 450 g (1 lb)	*Position* thicker parts towards the outside of the dish. *Turn* halfway through cooking if steaks are thick.
Skate wings	6–7 minutes on HIGH per 450 g (1 lb)	*Add* 150 ml (¼ pint) stock or milk. If cooking more than 900 g (2 lb) cook in batches.
Smoked fish	Cook as appropriate for type of fish, e.g. whole, fillet or cutlet. See above.	
Squid	Put prepared squid, cut into rings in a large bowl with 150 ml (¼ pint) wine, stock or water per 450 g (1 lb) of squid. Cook, covered, on HIGH for 5–8 minutes per 450 g (1 lb)	*Time* depends on size of squid – larger, older, squid are tougher and may take longer to cook.
Octopus	Put prepared octopus, cut into 2.5 cm (1 inch) pieces, in a large bowl with 150 ml (¼ pint) wine, stock or water per 450 g (1 lb) of octopus. Cook, covered on HIGH until liquid is boiling, then on MEDIUM for 15–20 minutes per 450 g (1 lb)	*Tenderise* octopus before cooking by beating vigorously with a meat mallet or rolling pin. *Marinate* before cooking to help tenderise. Time depends on age and size of octopus.
Scallops (shelled)	2–4 minutes on HIGH per 450 g (1 lb)	Do not overcook or scallops will be tough. Add corals for 1–2 minutes at end of cooking time.
Scallops in their shells	Do not cook in the microwave	Cook conventionally.

Fish Cooking Chart ... contd.

Type	Time/Setting	Microwave Cooking Technique(s)
Mussels	Put up to 900 g (2 lb) mussels in a large bowl with 150 ml (¼ pint) wine, stock or water. Cook, covered, on HIGH for 3–5 minutes	*Remove* mussels on the top as they cook. *Shake* the bowl occasionally during cooking. *Discard* any mussels which do not open.
Cockles	Put cockles in a large bowl with a little water. Cook, covered, on HIGH for 3–4 minutes until the shells open. Take cockles out of their shells and cook for a further 2–3 minutes or until hot	Shake the bowl occasionally during cooking.
Oysters	Do not cook in the microwave	
Raw prawns	2–5 minutes on HIGH per 450 g (1 lb), stirring frequently	Time depends on the size of the prawns. *Cook* until their colour changes to bright pink.
Live lobster	Do not cook in the microwave	Cook conventionally.
Live crab	Do not cook in the microwave	Cook conventionally.
Small clams	Cook as mussels	As mussels.
Large clams	Do not cook in the microwave	Cook conventionally.

FLOWERS

Q *I've heard you can dry flowers in the microwave to make pot pourri. Is this true?*

A Yes. You can dry flowers in the microwave but individual petals will dry more successfully than whole flower heads.

To dry petals, arrange them in a single layer on a piece of absorbent kitchen paper. Cook on HIGH for 1 minute. Turn the petals over and reposition and cook for a further 1 minute until the petals are dry. Turn into a bowl and add a few drops of pot pourri revitaliser to add the perfume of your choice.

FOIL

Q *I've noticed in some of my cookery books that foil is recommended. Is it safe to use and do you recommend it?*

A Foil used to be recommended in microwave cookery for shielding parts of food but I no longer suggest it. This is because it must be used very carefully, for example, in only small smooth pieces otherwise it causes Arcing. I also don't think it's necessary. After all, you wouldn't shield a fish tail or the end of a bone of meat if you were cooking it conventionally.

FOOD TEMPERATURE

Q *If I take food straight out of the refrigerator, will it take longer to cook than if it were at room temperature?*

A Yes. The initial temperature of the food to be cooked will affect the cooking and reheating times of all foods. Food cooked straight from the refrigerator will therefore take longer than food at room temperature.

FRUIT

Q *Should I add water to fruit when cooking it in the microwave?*

A Fruit with a high water content, such as rhubarb, will need no additional water, but a small quantity of water is required when stewing hard fruits, such as apples and plums. A rough guide is 45–60 ml (3–4 tbsp) water to 450 g (1 lb) fruit. Soft fruits, such as blackberries and raspberries, do not generally require any additional water:

FRUIT

Apples

Q *Can I bake apples in the microwave?*

A Yes. Nothing could be simpler, but remember to cut the skins around the middle first, to prevent them from bursting. Four medium cooking apples, cored and stuffed and cooked on HIGH, will take 5–7 minutes.

Oranges and Lemons

Q *I've been told you can get more juice out of oranges and lemons by putting them in the microwave. Is this possible?*

A Yes. To release the maximum of squeezed juice from citrus fruits, cook on HIGH for 1–2 minutes.

FRYING

Q *Is it possible to shallow or deep fry in a microwave cooker?*

A No. Shallow or deep frying should never be attempted in a microwave cooker. However, by using a browning dish or skillet a similar result can often be achieved. Alternatively, see STIR-FRYING, page 122.

FUDGE

Q *Can I make fudge in the microwave?*

A Yes, and here is a very quick and easy chocolate fudge recipe. Simply put 100 g (4 oz) each of butter and plain chocolate, 450 g (1 lb) icing sugar and 45 ml (3 tbsp) milk in a large heatproof bowl. Cook on HIGH for 3 minutes until the chocolate has melted then beat vigorously with a wooden spoon until thick and creamy. Pour into a shallow container and leave until set. Cut into squares when cold.

G

GARLIC BREAD

Q *Can I cook garlic bread in the microwave?*

A Yes, it works very well and is delicious but the result is obviously soft compared to the crisp crust you get when it is baked conventionally. This is how you make it in the microwave.

50 g (2 oz) butter or margarine
1 garlic clove, skinned and crushed
salt and pepper
1 small baguette

1 Put the butter or margarine into a small bowl and cook on HIGH for 10–30 seconds or until just soft enough to spread. Beat in the garlic and season to taste with salt and pepper.

2 Cut the bread into 2.5 cm (1 inch) slices and spread each slice with the butter. Stick the slices back together to re-form the loaf.

3 Wrap in greaseproof paper and cook on HIGH for 1–2 minutes or until the bread is hot. Serve immediately.

GELATINE

Q *Can I dissolve gelatine in the microwave?*

A Yes. Sprinkle the gelatine into the measured cold water according to the packet instructions and leave to soak and swell for 1 minute. Cook on HIGH for 30–35 seconds until dissolved, stirring frequently. Do not boil.

GINGERBREAD

GINGERBREAD

Q *Can I bake my favourite gingerbread in the microwave?*

A Because gingerbreads are temperamental, even when baked conventionally, it is probably best to bake it in your oven as usual. However, you can save time and washing up by melting the butter, treacle, milk and sugar in a large, heatproof bowl on HIGH for about 4 minutes. Try this for other melting method cakes too.

GLASS

Q *Is it true that I can use glass other than ovenproof glass in the microwave?*

A Glass allows the microwaves to pass through the dish so it remains cool in areas that are not in contact with food, but during cooking areas of the container that are next to the food will become hot due to the conduction of heat. Therefore, ordinary glasses are only suitable for short term heating of foods with a low sugar or fat content. Do not use cut glass or leaded glass.

GOLDEN SYRUP

Q *My syrup has crystallised. Is it possible to restore it in the microwave?*

A Yes. You can restore the texture of syrup that has crystallised by transferring it to a bowl and cooking on HIGH for 1–2 minutes.

GRILL see BROWNING ELEMENT

H

HERBS

Q *Is it possible to dry herbs in the microwave?*

A Yes, very successfully. You will need fresh herbs. Parsley, basil, rosemary and coriander are ideal, but any will do.

To dry herbs, strip the leaves of the herbs off their stems and arrange them in a single layer on a piece of absorbent kitchen paper. Cook on HIGH for 1 minute. Turn the leaves over and reposition and cook for a further 1–1½ minutes until the leaves are dry. (You can tell when they are dry because they will crumble when rubbed between the fingers.) Store in an airtight jar in a dark place.

HOLLANDAISE

Q *Can I make a hollandaise sauce successfully in the microwave?*

A Yes. If you follow these instructions exactly you will achieve perfect results every time.

100 g (4 oz) butter, cut into small pieces
2 egg yolks
30 ml (2 tbsp) white wine vinegar
white pepper

1 Put the butter in a large glass bowl and cook on HIGH for 30–60 seconds until just melted (do not cook for any longer or the butter will be too hot and the mixture will curdle).

2 Add the egg yolks and the vinegar and whisk together until well mixed. Cook on HIGH for 1–1½ minutes, whisking every 15 seconds until thick enough to coat the back of a spoon. Season with a little pepper and serve warm.

HONEY

Q *Is it possible to restore the texture of honey that has crystallised, in the microwave?*

A Yes. Cook the honey on HIGH for 1–2 minutes in its glass jar without the lid.

HOT AND COLD SPOTS

Q *I've heard the terms hot spots and cold spots. What exactly are these?*

A Some cookers have hot or cold spots. These are areas where food will cook at a faster or slower rate than elsewhere in the cooker. To overcome these, food should be repositioned during cooking.

I J K L

ICE CREAM

Q *I've heard that you can soften ice cream in the microwave. How do you do it?*

A The microwave is very good for softening rock hard ice cream but obviously it shouldn't be overheated or it will melt! Take the ice cream straight from the freezer then cook on LOW. (A 1 litre (1¾ pint) tub will take about 2 minutes.)

JELLY

Q *Can I dissolve jelly cubes in the microwave?*

A Yes. Simply put the jelly cubes in a jug or a bowl with 150 ml (¼ pint) cold water. Cook on HIGH for 1½–2½ minutes until melted, then stir until completely dissolved.

KEBABS

Q *Can I cook kebabs in the microwave?*

A Yes, very successfully, but remember to use wooden kebab sticks, and not metal skewers, to prevent arcing (see page 11). Because the kebabs will not brown, it is best for marinated chicken, fish or vegetables.

KIDNEYS see OFFAL

LIVER see OFFAL

M

MAGNETRON

Q *What exactly is a magnetron in a microwave cooker?*

A This is one of a microwave cooker's major components and its function is to convert the electric current into microwaves within the cavity of the cooker.

MARZIPAN

Q *Can I soften shop-bought marzipan in the microwave?*

A Yes. Simply remove the foil packaging, place the marzipan on a piece of absorbent kitchen paper and cook on HIGH for 1½-2 minutes or until soft and pliable.

MEAT

Q *Can you give me some hints for thawing meat successfully in the microwave?*

A ● As frozen meat gives off a lot of liquid during thawing and because microwaves are attracted to water, the liquid should be poured off or mopped up with absorbent kitchen paper when it collects, otherwise thawing will take longer.

● Start thawing a joint in its wrapper and remove it as soon as possible – usually after one-quarter of the thawing time. Place the joint on a microwave roasting rack so that it does not stand in liquid during thawing.

● Remember to turn over a large piece of meat during thawing.

● If the joint shows signs of cooking, give the meat a 'rest' period of 20 minutes.

- A joint is thawed when a skewer can easily pass through the thickest part of the meat.

- Chops and steaks should be repositioned during thawing. Test them by pressing the surface with your fingers – the meat should feel cold to the touch and give slightly in the thickest part.

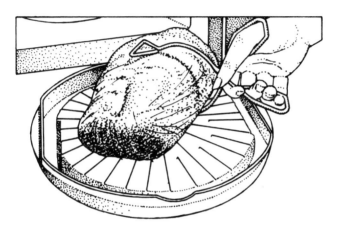

Turning joint over.

Q *Can you give me the times for thawing various cuts of meat in the microwave?*

A The following chart will help you.

Type	Time on LOW or DEFROST Setting	Notes
Beef		
Boned roasting joints (sirloin, topside)	8–10 minutes per 450 g (1 lb)	*Turn* over regularly during thawing and rest if the meat shows signs of cooking. *Stand* for 1 hour.

MEAT

Meat Thawing Times . . . contd.

Type	Time on LOW or DEFROST Setting	Notes
Joints on bone (rib of beef)	**10–12 minutes per 450 g (1 lb)**	*Turn* over joint during thawing. The meat will still be icy in the centre but will complete thawing if you leave it to stand for 1 hour.
Minced beef	8–10 minutes per 450 g (1 lb)	*Stand* for 10 minutes.
Cubed steak	6–8 minutes per 450 g (1 lb)	*Stand* for 10 minutes.
Steak (sirloin, rump)	8–10 minutes per 450 g (1 lb)	*Stand* for 10 minutes.
Lamb/Veal		
Boned rolled joint (loin, leg, shoulder)	5–6 minutes per 450 g (1 lb)	As for boned roasting joints of beef above. *Stand* for 30–45 minutes.
On the bone (leg and shoulder)	5–6 minutes per 450 g (1 lb)	As for beef joints on bone above. *Stand* for 30–45 minutes.
Minced lamb or veal	8–10 minutes per 450 g (1 lb)	*Stand* for 10 minutes.
Chops	8–10 minutes per 450 g (1 lb)	*Separate* during thawing. *Stand* for 10 minutes.
Pork		
Boned rolled joint (loin, leg)	7–8 minutes per 450 g (1 lb)	As for boned roasting joints of beef above. *Stand* for 1 hour.
On the bone (leg, hand)	7–8 minutes per 450 g (1 lb)	As for beef joints on bone above. *Stand* for 1 hour.
Tenderloin	8–10 minutes per 450 g (1 lb)	*Stand* for 10 minutes.
Chops	8–10 minutes per 450 g (1 lb)	*Separate* during thawing and arrange 'spoke' fashion. *Stand* for 10 minutes.
Offal		
Liver	8–10 minutes per 450 g (1 lb)	*Separate* during thawing. *Stand* for 5 minutes.
Kidney	6–9 minutes per 450 g (1 lb)	*Separate* during thawing. *Stand* for 5 minutes.

Q *Can you give me some hints for cooking meat successfully in the microwave?*

A
- Do not add salt directly on to meat before cooking as this draws out moisture and toughens the outside.

- Always ensure that joints of meat are completely thawed before cooking.

- Start cooking meat with the fatty side down. If it is more than 5 cm (2 inches) thick, turn it halfway through cooking.

- Cook meat in a roasting bag to improve browning.

- Position cuts of meat so that the thickest parts are pointing towards the edge of the dish.

- Arrange meatballs in a circle in a dish to ensure even cooking and try to leave a space in the middle so that microwaves can penetrate from the inner as well as the outer edges.

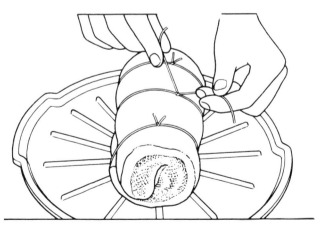

Regular-shaped joints cook most evenly.

- Regular-shaped joints of meat will cook more evenly than irregular joints, such as those that are boned or rolled.

- When roasting meat, use a microwave roasting rack or trivet to keep the juices from the underside of the meat and help the meat to brown.

- If using a meat thermometer, ensure that it is inserted into the thickest part of the joint and does not touch the bone in the meat.

Q *Can you tell me how long to cook the various types of meat in the microwave?*

A The following chart will help you.

Type	Time/Setting	Microwave cooking technique(s)
Beef		
Boned roasting joint (sirloin, topside)	per 450 g (1 lb) Rare: 5–6 minutes on HIGH Medium: 7–8 minutes on HIGH Well: 8–10 minutes on HIGH	*Turn* over joint halfway through cooking time. *Stand* for 15–20 minutes, tented in foil.
On the bone roasting joint (fore rib, back rib)	per 450 g (1 lb) Rare: 5 minutes on HIGH Medium: 6 minutes on HIGH Well: 8 minutes on HIGH	*Turn* over joint halfway through cooking time. *Stand* as for boned joint.
Lamb/Veal		
Boned rolled joint (loin, leg, shoulder)	per 450 g (1 lb) Medium: 7–8 minutes on HIGH Well: 8–10 minutes on HIGH	*Turn* over joint halfway through cooking time. *Stand* as for beef.
On the bone (leg and shoulder)	per 450 g (1 lb) Medium: 6–7 minutes on HIGH Well: 8–9 minutes on HIGH	*Position* fatty side down and turn over halfway through cooking time. *Stand* as for beef.

Meat Cooking Times ... contd.

ype	Time/Setting	Microwave cooking technique(s)
ˈhops	1 chop: 2½–3½ minutes on HIGH 2 chops: 3½–4½ minutes on HIGH 3 chops: 4½–5½ minutes on HIGH 4 chops: 5½–6½ minutes on HIGH	*Cook* in preheated browning dish. *Position* with bone ends towards centre. *Turn* over once during cooking.
ˈacon ɔints	12–14 minutes on HIGH per 450 g (1 lb)	*Cook* in a pierced roasting bag. *Turn* over joint partway through cooking time. *Stand* for 10 minutes, tented in foil.
ˈashers	2 rashers: 2–2½ minutes on HIGH 4 rashers: 4–4½ minutes on HIGH 6 rashers: 5–6 minutes on HIGH	*Arrange* in a single layer. *Cover* with greaseproof paper to prevent splattering. *Cook* in preheated browning dish if liked. *Remove* paper immediately after cooking to prevent sticking.
ˈork ˈoned rolled joint (loin, ˈg)	8–10 minutes on HIGH per 450 g (1 lb)	As for boned rolled lamb opposite.
ɔn the bone (leg, hand)	8–9 minutes on HIGH per 450 g (1 lb)	As for lamb on the bone opposite.
ˈhops	1 chop: 4–4½ minutes on HIGH 2 chops: 5–5½ minutes on HIGH 3 chops: 6–7 minutes on HIGH 4 chops: 6½–8 minutes on HIGH	*Cook* in preheated browning dish. *Prick* kidney, if attached. *Position* with bone ends towards centre. *Turn* over once during cooking.
ɔffal ˈiver (lamb and calves)	6–8 minutes on HIGH per 450 g (1 lb)	*Cover* with greaseproof paper to prevent splattering.

Meat Cooking Times ... contd.

Type	Time/Setting	Microwave cooking technique(s)
Kidneys	8 minutes on HIGH per 450 g (1 lb)	*Arrange* in a circle. *Cover* to prevent splattering. *Reposition* during cooking.

Bacon

Q *How do I cook bacon rashers in the microwave?*

A Remove the rind and snip the fat of the bacon with scissor to prevent it from curling up during cooking. Lay the bacon in a single layer on a roasting rack or large flat plate. Cove with absorbent kitchen paper to absorb the fat and preven it from splattering. Cook the bacon on HIGH until cooked. (rashers will take 2–2½ minutes, 4 rashers 4–4½ minutes, rashers 5–6 minutes.) Remove the paper quickly to preven it sticking to the bacon.

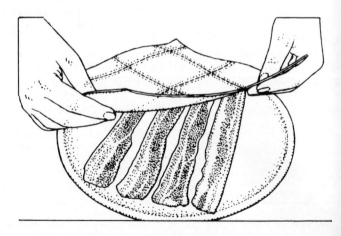

Covering bacon with absorbent kitchen paper.

MELBA TOAST

Q   *Can I make Melba toast in the microwave?*

A   Yes. Toast the bread on both sides, then using a sharp knife, slice the bread in half horizontally (to make two very thin slices). Place, untoasted side up, on a large plate or straight on the cooker base and cook on HIGH for 30–40 seconds until dry and crisp.

MERINGUES

Q   *Can I make meringues in the microwave?*

A   Conventional meringue mixture cannot be cooked in a microwave but by making a mixture similar to fondant the results are excellent. The mixture puffs up like magic and makes delicate meringues which can be topped with cream and fresh fruit. It makes rather a lot – if you prefer, some of the mixture may be tightly wrapped and stored in the refrigerator for about 2 weeks. Here is the recipe.

MICROWAVE MERINGUES

MAKES 32

1 egg white
about 275–300 g (10–11 oz) icing sugar
double cream, whipped
fresh fruit in season, such as strawberries, raspberries, kiwi fruit,
peaches

1   Put the egg white in a medium bowl and whisk lightly with a fork. Gradually sift in the icing sugar and mix to give a very firm, non-sticky but pliable dough.

2   Roll the mixture into small balls about the size of a walnut. Place a sheet of greaseproof paper in the base of the cooker or on the turntable and arrange eight balls of paste in a circle on the paper, spacing them well apart.

3   Cook on HIGH for 1½ minutes until the paste has puffed up and formed meringue-like balls.

4   Carefully lift the cooked meringues off the paper and transfer to a wire rack to cool. Repeat three more times with the remaining fondant to make 32 meringues.

5   Just before serving top the meringues with cream and fresh fruit.

MICROWAVE COOKERS

Q   *Why are microwaves sometimes called cookers and not ovens?*

A   You will see that I always refer to microwaves as cookers. I feel that this term is more appropriate than 'ovens' since, in addition to oven-type cooking, they can carry out tasks which are normally done on the hob such as boiling, poaching, melting, browning, pan and stir frying, steaming, softening, dissolving and making sauces.

Q   *Can you give me some hints on buying a microwave cooker?*

A   • Choose a microwave cooker with a wattage output of no less than 600–700 watts. A 500 watt-cooker may be less expensive but see COOKER SETTINGS for more information.

• Select one with a large cooker capacity or at least one that your dishes will fit into.

• Buy an established model name, within a range, for reliability.

• A microwave cooker with additional shelves may not be an advantage to you. (See SHELVING for more information.)

• A microwave cooker with a browning element or grill may also not be necessary for you. (See BROWNING ELEMENT for further information.)

- Choose a microwave cooker with controls that you find easy to use and understand. They may be mechanical or digital touch controls, which you probably pay more for.

- Temperature probes and automatic programming are useful to some cooks. See the individual entries in the book for further information on these and whether they would be useful to you.

- Whether you choose to buy a microwave cooker with a turntable or not is again a matter of personal preference. (See TURNTABLE and STIRRER for more advice.)

- The number of power settings varies between cookers and you may or may not find this useful for cooking. You will probably find that you only use three or four of the settings. (See also POWER SETTINGS.)

Q *Will my microwave cooker replace my conventional oven?*

A No. I don't see the microwave as an appliance to completely replace your conventional oven – because it has its limitations. There are certain foods that a conventional oven cooks better than a microwave, and there is also a limit to the amount of food you can put in a microwave at any one time. Nevertheless, the microwave also cooks some foods better than a conventional oven and, of course, its main advantage is speed. It is certainly an invaluable appliance to have.

Q *Is a microwave cooker cheaper or more expensive to use than a conventional oven?*

A Shorter cooking times and a lower electricity loading (1.5 kw compared with 3.5 kw for a conventional oven) usually means that a microwave cooker is cheaper to run.

Q *Why does the turntable of my cooker get hot sometimes? Is this anything to worry about?*

A The turntable of a microwave cooker can often get hot because heat transfers from the food to the part of the container it is in contact with. The heat from the container then heats the turntable. This is usually nothing to worry about unless of course the turntable becomes very hot which might cause it to break. If you think this may be happening, remove the dish from the cooker (using oven gloves) and allow it to cool. Leave the cooker door open to allow that to cool too. The same applies to glass shelves in the base of microwave cookers.

MICROWAVES

Q *What exactly are microwaves and how do they work?*

A Microwaves are electromagnetic waves of energy similar to TV transmitters. They penetrate food to a depth of 5 cm (2 inches) where they are absorbed by water molecules. When this happens the molecules vibrate at great speed. This movement generates heat by friction (like two sticks being rubbed together) and cooks the food in a very short time.

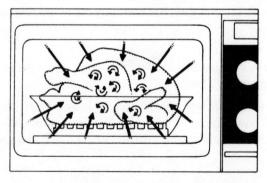

Vibrating molecules produce heat.

MICROWAVE THERMOMETER

Q *What is a microwave thermometer?*

A This is useful for cooking meat in cookers not equipped with a temperature probe and replaces a conventional meat thermometer which because of its mercury content cannot be used in a microwave cooker. A conventional meat thermometer should only be used *after* food is cooked.

N

NAPKINS

Q *Is it true that you can use napkins in the microwave?*

A Yes. Cotton, linen and paper napkins can be used for briefly warming bread rolls. Do make sure, though, that they are made of pure fibres and contain no synthetic properties.

NUTRITIVE VALUE

Q *What happens to the nutritional value of vitamins and minerals in foods when cooked in the microwave?*

A
- Water-soluble vitamin C and B-group vitamins are easily destroyed during any form of cooking but cooking in the microwave does minimise vitamin and mineral losses. This is because the foods are cooked quickly in small amounts of water or in their own juices, which means there is less likelihood that vitamins and minerals will leach out and be lost in the cooking water.

- The nutritional value of food will of course be less when you reheat it.

NUTS

Q *Can I brown nuts in the microwave?*

A Yes. Spread 25–100 g (1–4 oz) flaked, or blanched almonds or hazelnuts on a large plate and cook on HIGH for 6–10 minutes, stirring very frequently, until lightly browned.

Spread out nuts on a plate or in a shallow dish.

Q *Can I blanch nuts in the microwave?*

A • Yes. To blanch almonds, put 100 g (4 oz) nuts in a bowl with 150 ml (¼ pint) water. Cook on HIGH for about 2 minutes. Drain and slip the skins off with your fingers.

• To blanch hazelnuts, place them in a single layer on absorbent kitchen paper and cook on high for 30 seconds. Tip the nuts on to a tea-towel and rub off the skins.

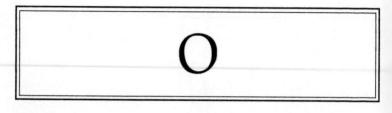

O

OFFAL

Kidneys

Q *How do I stop kidneys from popping and splattering all over the microwave during cooking?*

A Prick each kidney twice with a fork to prevent them popping during cooking. Alternatively, finely chop the kidneys. Covering them during cooking also helps!

Liver see **Kidneys**

ONIONS see VEGETABLES

ORANGES AND LEMONS see FRUIT

P

PANCAKES

Q *Can I reheat pancakes in the microwave?*

A Yes, interleave and cover the pancakes with greaseproof paper, up to eight at a time, then cook on HIGH for 1–1½ minutes or until warmed through.

PAPER

Q *Why do some recipes tell me to put the food on or cover it with absorbent kitchen paper?*

A Absorbent kitchen paper helps to absorb the moisture during cooking, as when baking potatoes. It will also absorb fat, as, for example, when cooking bacon.

PASTA

Q *Can you give me some hints for cooking pasta successfully in the microwave?*

A • Boil the water for cooking pasta in a kettle to save time.

• When cooking pasta always cover the container.

• Large quantities of pasta are better cooked conventionally.

• Remove the pasta from the cooker when it is still slightly undercooked, otherwise prolonged cooking will cause it to become soggy. Part of the cooking occurs during the standing time.

- Pasta should be covered and left to stand in its cooking liquid for 5–10 minutes, depending on the type of pasta shape (allow longer for larger pasta shapes). If you are making a sauce, do this during standing time.

- Frozen pasta can be cooked directly from frozen on the HIGH setting unless combined with a sauce which might spoil or curdle.

- Once pasta is tossed in a sauce it can be reheated quickly if necessary and will still retain its freshness.

Q *What is the best way to cook pasta in the microwave and how long should I allow?*

A Put the pasta and salt to taste in a large bowl. Pour over enough boiling water to cover the pasta by 2.5 cm (1 inch). Stir and cover then cook on HIGH for the stated time, stirring occasionally.

Type and Quantity	Time on HIGH Setting	Microwave Cooking Technique(s)
Fresh white/wholemeal/ spinach pasta 225 g (8 oz)	3–4 minutes	Stand for 5 minutes. Do not drain.
Dried white/wholemeal/ spinach pasta shapes 225 g (8 oz)	8–10 minutes	Stand for 5 minutes. Do not drain.
Dried white/wholemeal/ spinach pasta shapes 450 g (1 lb)	12–14 minutes	Stand for 5 minutes. Do not drain.
Dried white/wholemeal spaghetti 225 g (8 oz)	7–8 minutes	Stand for 5 minutes. Do not drain.
Dried white/wholemeal spaghetti 450 g (1 lb)	8–10 minutes	Stand for 5 minutes. Do not drain.

PASTRY

Q *How long does it take to thaw pastry in the microwave?*

A
- A 227 g (8 oz) packet of shortcrust or puff pastry should be thawed on the LOW or DEFROST setting for 1 minute then left to stand for 20 minutes.

- A 397 g (14 oz) packet of shortcrust or puff pastry should be thawed on the LOW or DEFROST setting for 2 minutes then left to stand for 20–30 minutes.

Q *Can I cook shortcrust pastry in the microwave?*

A It is possible but unless it is made with wholemeal flour it will be pale. Even a pale flan case, however, can look attractive once a filling is added. Also, the pastry will not be crisp, though rolling it out very thinly will achieve a crisper result. Here is a recipe for you to try; omit the sugar if you want a savoury flan case.

175 g (6 oz) plain wholemeal flour
pinch of salt
75 g (3 oz) butter or margarine
30 ml (2 level tbsp) light muscovado sugar (optional)

1 Grease a 20.5 cm (8 inch) fluted flan dish and line the base with greaseproof paper.

2 Put the flour and salt in a bowl and rub in the butter or margarine until the mixture resembles fine breadcrumbs. Mix in the sugar, if using. Add about 45 ml (3 tbsp) water to make a firm dough.

3 Turn on to a lightly-floured surface and knead for a few seconds until smooth. Roll out thinly and use to line the base and sides of the prepared flan dish. Prick the base and sides with a fork.

4 Cover loosely with kitchen paper, stand on a roasting rack and cook on HIGH for 6–7 minutes or until the pastry is firm to the touch and just shrinking away from the sides of the dish.

5   Leave to stand for 2–3 minutes, then carefully remove the pastry case from the dish. Remove the greaseproof paper and place on a large flat plate. Fill with the filling of your choice.

Q *Why does cooked pastry go soft when reheated in the microwave?*

A Microwaves are attracted to the moist fillings in pastries and pies, so that the liquid will heat up quickly. The steam produced by this is often absorbed into the pastry which may not leave it as crispy as that reheated in a conventional oven. For hints on reheating pastry, see REHEATING.

PEPPERS see VEGETABLES

PITTA BREAD

Q *Can I warm pitta bread in the microwave?*

A Yes, but only if you intend to eat it immediately, because when the bread cools it hardens! One large pitta bread takes about 15 seconds on HIGH.

PLATES

Q *Can I warm plates in the microwave?*

A You can, but I don't think it's worthwhile unless you really don't have any other way of warming plates. If you do want to warm them in the microwave, put a little water between the plates and on the top one. Heat on HIGH for 30 seconds–1 minute until warm.

POACHING AND STEAMING

Q *How do I poach or steam food in the microwave?*

A Chop into evenly sized pieces and place in a large, shallow dish. Add the amount of liquid stated in the recipe and cover with a tightly fitting lid or a heavy plate. Because food cooks in its own moisture, less liquid is needed than when poaching or steaming conventionally. Stir or re-position during cooking.

POPCORN

Q *Is it true that I can cook popcorn in the microwave?*

A Yes. Specially designed microwave popcorn poppers are available, but they're very expensive and not necessary – a large bowl and a lid or heavy plate works just as well. Look out, too, for bags containing popcorn and butter or salt flavourings manufactured for cooking in the microwave. They're great fun to watch as they puff up and fill with popped corn! Here is the recipe:

15 ml (1 tbsp) vegetable oil
75 g (3 oz) popping corn
salt

Put the oil in a very large heatproof bowl and cook on HIGH for 1–2 minutes or until hot. Stir in the corn, cover with a lid or heavy plate and cook on HIGH for 7 minutes or until the popping stops, shaking the bowl occasionally. Add salt to taste. Best eaten while still warm.

POPPADUMS

Q *Can I cook poppadums in the microwave?*

A Yes. Brush the number of poppadums required on one side, with a little oil. Then cook one poppadum at a time on HIGH for 1 minute or until crisp and puffed up all over.

POPPING

Q *Why do some foods 'pop' while cooking in the microwave?*

A This is because these foods have a skin or membrane, which bursts and 'pops' when heat builds up underneath it. All foods with a skin or membrane such as liver, kidneys and egg yolks, should be pricked with a fine skewer or the point of a sharp knife before cooking to prevent this from happening.

PORRIDGE

Q *Can I cook porridge in the microwave?*

A Yes, and not only is the result very good, but it also doesn't stick to the bowl! Here is the recipe.

SERVES 2

50 g (2 oz) porridge oats
300 ml (½ pint) milk

1   Put the oats and milk in a medium bowl. Cook on HIGH for 4–5 minutes until boiling and thickened, stirring every minute.

2   Stir in the flavouring of your choice such as honey, demerara sugar, chopped dried dates or prunes, nuts or salt and serve hot.

POTATOES see VEGETABLES

POULTRY AND GAME

Q *What is the best way to thaw poultry and game in the microwave?*

A Poultry or game should be thawed in its freezer wrapping which should be pierced first and the metal tag removed. During thawing in the microwave, pour off liquid that collects in the bag. Finish thawing in a bowl of cold water with the bird still in its bag. Chicken portions can be thawed in their polystyrene trays.

Q *How long does it take to thaw the various types of poultry and game in the microwave?*

A Follow the chart below for thawing times.

Type	Time on LOW or DEFROST **Setting**	Notes
Whole chicken or duckling	6–8 minutes per 450 g (1 lb)	Remove giblets. *Stand* in cold water for 30 minutes.
Whole turkey	10–12 minutes per 450 g (1 lb)	Remove giblets. *Stand* in cold water for 2–3 hours.
Chicken portions	5–7 minutes per 450 g (1 lb)	*Separate* during thawing. *Stand* for 10 minutes.
Poussin, grouse, pheasant, pigeon, quail	5–7 minutes per 450 g (1 lb)	

Q *How long does it take to cook the various types of poultry and game in the microwave?*

A Follow the chart below for the cooking times.

Type	Time/Setting	Microwave Cooking Technique(s)
Chicken Whole chicken	8–10 minutes on HIGH per 450 g (1 lb)	*Cook* in a roasting bag, breast side down and turn halfway through cooking. *Stand* for 10–15 minutes.

Poultry and Game Cooking Times ... contd.

Type	Time Setting	Microwave Cooking Technique(s)
Chicken continued		
Portions	6–8 minutes on HIGH per 450 g (1 lb)	*Position* skin side up with thinner parts towards the centre. *Reposition* halfway through cooking time. *Stand* for 5–10 minutes.
Boneless breast	2–3 minutes on HIGH	
Duck		
Whole	7–10 minutes on HIGH per 450 g (1 lb)	*Turn* over as for whole chicken. *Stand* for 10–15 minutes.
Portions	Four 300 g (11 oz) pieces: 10 minutes on HIGH then 30–35 minutes on MEDIUM	*Position* and *reposition* as for portions above.
Turkey		
Whole	9–11 minutes on HIGH per 450 g (1 lb)	*Turn* over three or four times, depending on size, during cooking: start cooking breast side down. *Stand* for 10–15 minutes.

Q *Can you give me some hints for cooking poultry and game in the microwave?*

A
- Roasting bags are useful for cooking poultry without spattering. Use an elastic band to secure them, not metal twist ties which could cause arcing. Pierce the bags before cooking to allow steam to escape.

- Boned and rolled poultry cooks more evenly because the shape and thickness are consistent.

- Arrange portions of poultry so that the thinnest parts are pointing towards the centre of the dish.

- Turn poultry portions over at least once during cooking to ensure that they cook evenly.

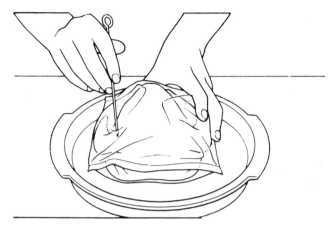

Cooking chicken in a roasting bag.

- Salt toughens poultry and makes it dry out if added directly on to the food without any liquid. It is therefore best to add it after cooking.

- When cooking duck, spoon off the fat during cooking to prevent a pool forming and spattering occurring, and cover with a split roasting bag.

- Poultry and game are cooked when a knife is inserted into the thickest part of the meat and the juices run clear.

Chicken

Q *Is it possible to roast a whole chicken in the microwave and if so, how do I do it?*

A It is possible, but because it cooks so quickly and the method of cooking uses moist rather than dry heat, the skin of the roast chicken will not be very brown, nor will it be crisp. Nevertheless, cooked this way it is ideal for salads, sandwiches or recipes requiring cooked chicken. Here are some hints to help brown the chicken followed by the recipe.

- To help it brown a little and to reduce splattering, cover with a split roasting bag.

- Commercially prepared browning agents are available, or paprika, honey, soy sauce and Worcestershire sauce may be brushed or sprinkled on to the skin before cooking.

- To achieve a brown and crisp skin, simply cook under a hot grill for a few minutes.

ROAST CHICKEN

1 oven-ready roasting chicken
salt and pepper
few fresh herbs (optional)
few lemon slices (optional)

1   Season the inside of the chicken with salt and pepper. Place herbs and lemon slices, if using, inside the chicken if wished.

2   Truss the chicken into a neat compact shape using fine string. Weigh the bird and calculate the cooking time allowing 8–10 minutes per 450 g (1 lb).

3   Stand the bird on a microwave roasting rack or trivet, breast side down, and stand the rack in a shallow dish to catch the juices. Cover with a split roasting bag and cook for half of the calculated time.

4   Turn over, re-cover and continue to cook for the remaining time.

5   Cover tightly with foil and leave to stand for 10 minutes before serving.

6   Brown and crisp under a hot grill, if liked.

Duck

Q *Can I roast a duck in the microwave?*

A Yes, see CHICKEN (page 103), but allow 7–9 minutes per 450 g (1 lb) for roasting duckling.

POWER OUTPUT

Q *What does power output mean?*

A This refers to the wattage of the cooker. Refer to your manufacturer's handbook to find the power output of your cooker.

POWER SETTINGS

Q *Why are there so many power settings on microwave cookers?*

A Unlike conventional ovens, microwave cookers are not standardised, which means that the power output and heat settings can vary tremendously between models. Settings in particular will vary and can be described in a number of different ways such as HIGH, MEDIUM, LOW, graduated numbers or terms such as Roast, Bake, Simmer, Defrost, Reheat.

PRESERVES

Q *Can you give me some hints for making preserves in the microwave?*

A • Only use your microwave for making a small quantity of preserve. The microwave is therefore particularly useful for preparing preserves if you only have a small batch of fruit or vegetables.

• Always use a large bowl to prevent the liquid from boiling over.

• Use a container made of a material which withstands the high temperature of boiling sugar.

PRESERVES

- Fruit skins such as lemon, orange and grapefruit tend to remain firm when cooked. For more tender skins, grate or chop the rind finely before using.

- Remember to handle bowls with oven gloves as they become hot during the cooking due to the conduction of heat from the food.

- Setting point of jams and marmalade is reached when a small spoonful of jam or marmalade placed on a cold saucer wrinkles when pushed with the tip of a finger.

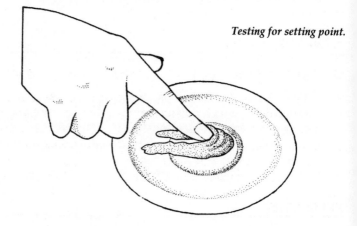

Testing for setting point.

- Less liquid may be required when cooking chutney because there is less evaporation.

- Cook chutneys until there is no pool of liquid on the surface and the mixture is thick.

- Never leave a thermometer in the container during cooking, unless it is especially made for microwave use.

- Never cover the container when cooking preserves unless instructions are given to the contrary.

- Use the microwave to sterilise jam jars. (See STERILISING.)

PULSES

Q *Can I cook pulses in the microwave and, if so, how long should I cook them?*

A The pulses in the chart below will cook successfully in the microwave cooker, making considerable time savings on conventional cooking. However, pulses with very tough skins, such as red kidney beans, black beans, butter beans, cannellini beans, haricot beans and soya beans will not cook in less time and are better cooked conventionally. Large quantities of all pulses are best cooked conventionally.

To cook pulses, soak beans overnight, then drain and cover with enough boiling water to come about 2.5 cm (1 inch) above the level of the beans. Cover and cook on HIGH for the time stated below, stirring occasionally.

Type 225 g (8 oz) quantity	Time on HIGH Setting	Microwave Cooking Technique(s)
Aduki beans	30–35 minutes	Stand for 5 minutes. Do not drain.
Black-eye beans	25–30 minutes	Stand for 5 minutes. Do not drain.
Chick peas	50–55 minutes	Stand for 5 minutes. Do not drain.
Flageolet beans	40–45 minutes	Stand for 5 minutes. Do not drain.
Mung beans	30–35 minutes	Stand for 5 minutes. Do not drain.
Split peas/lentils (do not need overnight soaking)	25–30 minutes	Stand for 5 minutes. Do not drain.

Q

QUANTITIES

Q *When I cook a larger or smaller quantity than that specified in the recipe, how much more, or less, time should I allow?*

A As a general guide:

- When doubling the ingredients, allow about one third to one half extra cooking time.

- When halving the ingredients, decrease the cooking time by slightly more than half the time allowed.

R

REHEATING

Q *Is the microwave a safe method of reheating food?*

A Yes. It is probably the safest way to reheat foods because the high internal temperatures reached reduce many of the health risks that are associated with slower reheating methods.

Q *Can you give me some hints for successfully reheating food in the microwave?*

A • Follow the same procedure as when reheating foods conventionally and cover foods such as vegetables to prevent them drying out. Stir the food occasionally for even heating: items that cannot be stirred should be turned or rearranged.

• Reheating in a microwave is extremely quick so special attention should be given to small items of food to avoid overcooking.

• Special attention must be paid to cooked pastry and breads. Place these on absorbent kitchen paper to absorb moisture during reheating and prevent the bottom from becoming soggy.

• Fat and sugar attract microwaves and tend to cook before other ingredients. Beware, for example, of fillings in sweet pies, as these can be considerably hotter than the rest of the dish.

• When reheating an entire meal on the same plate, keep the height of the various items as even as possible and arrange the more dense and thicker items towards the outside of the plate.

Q *How long should I reheat food for?*

A Only general guidelines for reheating food can be given as so much will depend on the type of food and the initial temperature of the food you are reheating. As a general rule, for an individual serving, try starting with 2 minutes on HIGH, test to see if the food is hot and then repeat in 2-minute bursts if it is not. With pastry foods such as fruit pies, the outer pastry should feel just warm. The temperature of pastry and filling will equalise if given a few minutes' standing time.

Q *Can I reheat more than one food at a time in the microwave?*

A Yes, but the food should be about the same size and density so that they cook evenly.

RICE

Q *Please can you give me some hints for cooking rice in the microwave?*

A ● Boil the water for cooking rice in a kettle to save time.

● Always cover the container when cooking rice.

● Large quantities of rice are best cooked by the conventional method.

Q *What is the best method for cooking rice and how long should I cook it for?*

A The best method is to put the rice and salt to taste in a large bowl then pour over enough boiling water to cover the rice by 2.5 cm (1 inch). Stir and cover the bowl, then cook on HIGH for the stated time, stirring occasionally.

Type	Quantity	Time on HIGH Setting
White rice	225 g (8 oz)	10–12 minutes
Brown rice	225 g (8 oz)	30–35 minutes

Q *Can I reheat rice in the microwave?*

A Yes, it reheats very well. This is particularly useful if you want to serve rice at a dinner party, but are nervous about cooking it at the last moment. Simply cook the rice in advance, drain, rinse in cold water then turn into a serving dish. To reheat, dot with butter, cover and cook on HIGH for 2–4 minutes or until hot, stirring once.

RING MOULD

Q *I haven't got a ring mould. Can you suggest an alternative?*

A Yes, you can improvise a ring mould by placing an upturned heavy tumbler in the middle of a flat bottomed dish (a soufflé dish is ideal).

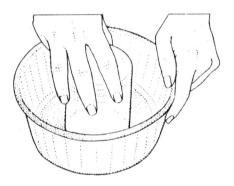

Making a ring mould.

ROASTING

Q *Can I roast meat in the microwave?*

A Large joints of meat cannot be cooked in a microwave because the microwaves cannot reach the centre of the joint without the outside being overcooked. Small joints, however, can be cooked by this method.

Q *Can you give me some hints for successfully roasting meat in the microwave?*

A ● Boned and rolled meats cook more evenly when roasted in the microwave because the shape and thickness are uniform.

● When roasting meat, use a microwave roasting rack or trivet to keep the juices from the underside of the meat and help the meat to brown.

● For even cooking, joints of meat should be uncovered and then turned at least once during cooking.

● Season meat at the end of cooking, never before, because salt drains out the moisture from the meat and makes it dry.

● When roasting joints of meat, standing time must often be allowed. Remove the roast from the cooker, cover or wrap it in foil and leave to stand for the time specified in the recipe.

ROASTING RACK

Q *What is a microwave roasting rack?*

A This is a rack specially designed for use in the microwave. It is not only useful for elevating meat and poultry above their own juices during cooking, but is also ideal for baking. If a cake is placed on one, the microwaves can circulate underneath the container and will allow the cake to cook more evenly.

SAFETY

Q *Is the microwave safe for children to use?*

A The absence of direct heat or gas burners and the automatic switching off when the cooker door is opened, means it is the safest cooking method for children to use. However, because the dishes can get hot, they should be taught to use oven gloves.

Q *Is it safe to stand near microwave cookers or can they harm you in any way?*

A There is no need to be worried about the safety of microwave cookers. Microwaves are not produced unless the door is closed and the doors are fitted with special door locks, door seals and safety cut-out micro-switches that automatically switch the power off as soon as the door is opened. The cookers are also effectively sealed against the leakage of microwaves as they are built to very precise specifications. It is therefore not harmful to stand in front of or near a microwave cooker.

Q *Why don't microwaves escape through the glass door of the cooker?*

A The cooker doors have a specially designed fine mesh through which the microwaves cannot escape. They simply bounce off the mesh and around the cavity until they are absorbed by the food, or the cooker door is opened and the microwave switches off. It is therefore quite safe to watch the food while it is cooking.

Q *Does it matter if my microwave is turned on and there is nothing in it?*

A If the cavity is empty when the cooker is switched on the component parts may be damaged. As a precautionary measure, keep a cup of water in the cooker when it is not being used for cooking just in case the cooker is accidentally switched on.

Q *How often should I have my microwave cooker checked?*

A If you use your cooker correctly and do not move it about frequently or drop it, there's no need for it to be checked and it will give you years of service. If, however, a service on your microwave is required, it should only be carried out by a qualified engineer from the manufacturing company.

SALT

Q *If cooking in a microwave, when is the best time to season the food with salt?*

A Salt, if sprinkled directly on foods such as meat, fish and vegetables, toughens and makes them dry out. It is therefore best to add it after cooking.

SAUCES

Q *Could you give me some hints for making sauces successfully in the microwave?*

A • Always use a container large enough to prevent the sauce from boiling over.

• Whisk sauces frequently during cooking to prevent lumps forming.

• When making sauces thickened with cornflour or arrowroot, make sure the thickening agent is completely dissolved in cold liquid before adding a hot one.

Use a whisk to prevent lumps forming.

- Sauces thickened with egg are best cooked on a LOW setting as care is needed to prevent them curdling.

- Frozen sauces can be reheated straight from the freezer. Transfer to a bowl then reheat, stirring to break up any frozen lumps.

Q *Can I make a white sauce in the microwave and if so, how?*

A A basic white sauce is wonderful cooked in a microwave. It is quick and simple to make because you use the all-in-one method. The secret for success is to whisk every minute, then you can guarantee a smooth sauce. Here is the recipe.

Pouring sauce:
15 g (½ oz) butter or margarine
15 g (½ oz) plain flour
300 ml (½ pint) milk
salt and pepper

Coating sauce:
25 g (1 oz) butter or margarine
25 g (1 oz) plain flour
300 ml (½ pint) milk
salt and pepper

1 Put all the ingredients in a medium bowl and whisk together.

2 Cook on HIGH for 4–5 minutes or until the sauce has boiled and thickened, whisking every minute. Season to taste with salt and pepper.

SAUSAGES

Q *Can I cook sausages in the microwave?*

A Although it is possible to cook sausages in a microwave, they don't look very appetising. Their colour can be improved by using a browning dish but even then it is only possible to cook four at a time. For this reason I wouldn't recommend it.

SCONES

Q *Can I warm scones in the microwave?*

A Yes, but this only works for small quantities, and if you like scones with a soft crust. Wrap the scones loosely in a napkin or absorbent kitchen paper and cook on HIGH in 1 minute bursts or until just warm. Eat immediately or they will become hard.

STEAMING see POACHING AND STEAMING

STEWING AND BRAISING

Q *How do I stew or braise food in the microwave?*

A Conventionally cooked stews and braises depend on long,

slow cooking to tenderise tough cuts of meat and allow the flavours to develop. For this reason, there is little point in using the microwave for this type of cooking. Instead, use it for stews made with tender cuts of meat, poultry and vegetables which do not need tenderising.

Here are some hints for successful microwave stewing and braising.

- Cut meat and vegetables into evenly sized pieces to ensure even cooking.

- Add less liquid than usual because foods cook in their own moisture.

- Cover the container with a large heavy plate or lid to prevent evaporation.

- Stir the stew or braise regularly throughout the cooking time to ensure even cooking.

- If the food cannot be stirred (chicken portions, chops etc) then reposition halfway through the cooking time instead.

SHELVING

Q Do you think it's a good idea to buy a microwave cooker with shelving in it?

A No, because shelving in a microwave significantly increases the volume of food in the cavity. This then increases the cooking time, thus reducing the benefit of speed.

SHOE POLISH

Q Is it true that the texture of shoe polish can be restored in the microwave?

A Yes, but don't put it in the microwave if it's in a metal container. Put the polish in the microwave, without its lid, and cook on HIGH in bursts of 30 seconds until the polish has softened.

SOUPS

Q *Do you have any hints for cooking soups in the microwave?*

A • Use a deep round container that allows plenty of room for the expansion of the liquid as it comes to the boil and for it to be stirred.

 • Although freshly microwaved soups are tasty, they will actually improve in flavour if made in advance, refrigerated for several hours and then reheated.

 • Use hot stock in preference to cold.

 • Soups can be reheated in individual bowls, so saving on washing up. Reheat soups on a LOW setting if they contain cream, seafood, mushrooms or pulses but use a HIGH setting for all others.

 • Pour soup that is to be frozen into single-portion containers so that it can be thawed in the microwave more quickly than a large quantity.

 • When reheating soups, stir several times to ensure even heating.

STANDING TIME

Q *What does 'standing time' mean in microwave cookery?*

A This term is often over-emphasised and only applies to certain foods such as meat joints, poultry and cakes. Standing time is an essential part of the cooking process in which the food is usually left to stand after it has been removed from the cooker. Although the food is no longer being cooked by microwave energy during standing time, the cooking is being completed by the conduction of the heat existing in the food to the centre (if standing time were incorporated into the microwave cooking time, the outside of the food would be overcooked while the centre remained uncooked). This is because microwave energy cooks from the outside in towards the centre. Standing time will depend on the density and size of the food. Very often (as in the case of potatoes) it will take no longer than the time taken to serve the dish. However, for large joints of meat, poultry and cakes, standing time could be up to ten minutes; this time should always be followed when specified in a recipe. Meat should be wrapped in foil during standing time to keep in the heat.

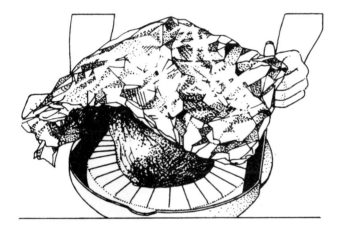

Wrap and leave to stand.

Q *Is it safe to eat food during its recommended standing time?*

A Yes, see the question above.

Q *Is it all right to leave foods in the microwave during the recommended standing time or should the foods be removed from the microwave?*

A As long as the cooker is switched off, it doesn't matter where you leave the food during the standing time.

STEAMED PUDDINGS

Q *Is it true that steamed puddings are good cooked in the microwave?*

A Yes. Both steamed sponge and suet puddings cook in a fraction of the time needed for conventional steaming and the results are excellent. To cook Roly-Poly suet puddings, follow your favourite recipe, wrap loosely in a large sheet of greaseproof paper, allowing room for expansion. Pleat the open ends tightly together and twist the ends to seal. Stand the parcel on a roasting rack and cook on HIGH for 4–5 minutes or until firm to the touch. Here is a basic sponge pudding recipe with some variations for you to try.

SPONGE PUDDING

SERVES 3–4

50 g (2 oz) soft tub margarine
50 g (2 oz) caster sugar
1 egg, beaten
few drops of vanilla flavouring
100 g (4 oz) self raising flour
45–60 ml (3–4 tbsp) milk

1 Beat the margarine, sugar, egg, vanilla flavouring and flour until smooth. Gradually stir in enough milk to give a soft dropping consistency.

2 Spoon into a greased 600 ml (1 pint) pudding basin and level the surface.

3 Cook on HIGH for 5–7 minutes until the top of the sponge is only slightly moist and a skewer inserted in the centre comes out clean.

4 Leave to stand for 5 minutes before turning out on to a warmed serving dish. Serve with custard.

Variations

Essex pudding
Spread jam over the sides and base of the greased pudding basin.

Apricot sponge pudding
Drain a 411 g (14½ oz) can of apricot halves and arrange them in the base of the greased pudding basin.

Syrup sponge pudding
Put 30 ml (2 tbsp) golden syrup into the bottom of the basin before adding the mixture. Flavour the mixture with the grated rind of a lemon.

Chocolate sponge pudding
Blend 60 ml (4 level tbsp) cocoa powder to a smooth cream with 15 ml (1 tbsp) hot water and add to the beaten ingredients.

Jamaica pudding
Add 50–100 g (2–4 oz) chopped stem ginger with the milk.

Lemon or orange sponge pudding
Add the grated rind of 1 orange or lemon when beating the ingredients.

Q *How do I tell when a steamed pudding is cooked?*

A To test when a sponge pudding is cooked, it should be slightly moist on the top and a skewer inserted in the centre should come out clean.

STERILISING

Q *Is it possible to sterilise jam jars, for preserves, in the microwave?*

A Yes, quarter fill up to four jars with water. Arrange in a circle in the cooker then bring to the boil on HIGH. Using oven gloves, remove each jar as it is ready and pour out the water. Invert the jar on a clean tea-towel or kitchen paper and use as required.

STIR-FRYING

Q *Can I cook stir-fried dishes in the microwave?*

A Yes, stir-fried dishes adapt well to the microwave cooker because only a small quantity of fat is used.

- Choose foods that cook quickly such as tender cuts of meat, chicken and vegetables.

- Cut the food to be cooked into small even-sized pieces for even cooking.

- Always use a large bowl or a large round shallow dish so that the foods cook more evenly.

- Add foods that cook more quickly last.

- If the dish contains spices these should be fried for 1–2 minutes, as they are conventionally, to release their flavour.

- Stir frequently, moving the food from the outside of the dish towards the centre to ensure even cooking.

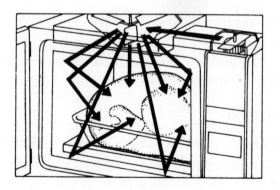

Built-in stirrers circulate microwaves.

122

STIRRER

Q *What is a stirrer?*

A This has the same effect as a turntable, and circulates the microwaves evenly throughout the cooker. Most microwave cookers have a built-in 'stirrer' positioned behind a splatter guard or cover in the roof of the cavity.

Stir during cooking.

STIRRING

Q *Does food need to be stirred during cooking in the microwave?*

A Yes. This is the most important technique in microwave cooking to ensure even cooking. Since the outer edges of food normally cook first in a microwave cooker, stir from the outside of the dish towards the centre. Foods that cannot be stirred should be turned over at least once during cooking.

SUGAR

Q *I've heard you can soften sugar that has become hard, in the microwave. Is this true?*

A Yes. Soften sugar that has become hard in its original wrapping on HIGH for 30–40 seconds.

SWEETS

Q *Can I make sweets in the microwave, and if so, how?*

A Yes you can and the same principles of making sweets conventionally apply when making them in the microwave. Here are some general hints to help you.

- Use a large heatproof bowl as the container can become very hot due to its high sugar content.

- With sugar and syrup-based sweets, make only the quantity given in the recipe and no more, to avoid boiling over.

- Never cover the container unless instructions are given to the contrary.

- Use oven gloves when handling the bowl as it can become very hot due to the conduction of heat from the mixture.

- Stir the hot mixture with a long wooden spoon to avoid being splattered.

- Watch chocolate carefully – if left too long in the microwave it will scorch.

- Do not use a conventional sugar boiling thermometer but test the mixture by dropping a small ball of the mixture in a glass of cold water to determine which stage the sugar has reached.

- Do not leave the mixture unattended while it is in the microwave cooker.

See also FUDGE, page 74.

T

TEMPERATURE PROBE

Q *What is a temperature probe?*

A A temperature probe or food sensor is used to cook joints of meat and poultry in the microwave, and enables you to control cooking by the internal temperature of the food, rather than by time. The probe is inserted into the thickest part of the food being cooked and the other end is plugged into a special socket in the cooker cavity. The desired temperature is then selected, according to the manufacturer's instructions. When the internal temperature reaches the pre-set level, the cooker switches itself off. It is, however, important that the probe be inserted in the thickest part of the flesh and not near a bone as it will give a misleading temperature reading. For this reason conventional thermometers inserted after cooking or conventional techniques for testing if food is cooked, are usually more reliable than probes or food sensors.

TENTING

Q *What does the term 'tenting' mean?*

A This term is used for covering cooked meats and poultry with foil, to retain the heat, during the standing time.

THAWING

Q *What is the best way to thaw food in the microwave?*

A When thawing in a microwave it is essential that the ice is melted slowly, so that the food does not begin to cook on the outside before it is completely thawed through to the centre. To prevent this happening, food must be allowed to 'rest' between bursts of microwave energy. This is especially important with large items. An AUTO DEFROST setting does this automatically by pulsing the energy on and off, but it can be done manually if your cooker does not have an automatic defrost control, by using the LOW or DEFROST setting. To speed up the thawing of food such as soups and stews, break them up during thawing.

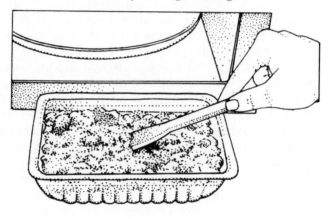

Break food up to thaw.

TURNTABLE

Q *Is it important to have a turntable in my microwave?*

A To ensure even cooking, food must be turned and a turntable does this automatically. However, even with a turntable, food must be re-positioned by hand to ensure even cooking. Some cookers are also equipped with automatic stirrers which are situated in the roof of the microwave. These will have the same effect as a turntable as they circulate the microwaves evenly throughout the cooker.

If you buy a microwave with a turntable, make sure that your dishes are not so large that they prevent the turntable from turning!

Rearranging small foods.

Q *Can I buy a separate turntable for my microwave?*

A Yes, but please see the preceding question before you rush out and buy one!

V

VEGETABLES

Q *What is the best way to cook vegetables in the microwave?*

A You may find these hints helpful.

- Cut vegetables into uniformly sized pieces so that they cook evenly.

- Arrange vegetables such as cauliflower and broccoli sprigs with the thickest part pointing towards the edge of the dish, for even cooking.

- Always pierce whole vegetables with skins, such as potatoes to prevent them bursting.

- Always stir vegetables or rearrange them halfway through cooking.

- When cooking whole vegetables, such as potatoes in their skins, arrange them in a circle with a space between each. Avoid putting one in the centre.

- To ensure even cooking, turn large vegetables such as potatoes and whole cauliflower over at least once during cooking.

- Unless instructions are given to the contrary, always cover the container.

- Season vegetables with salt after cooking if required as salt added before distorts the microwave patterns and dries out the vegetables.

- Frozen vegetables need no added liquid. Fresh vegetables require a small amount of water to create steam for cooking.

- Small frozen vegetables such as peas, sweetcorn kernels and mixed vegetables can be cooked in their plastic packets because the melting ice within the packet produces sufficient moisture for cooking. Split the top of the packet and shake it about halfway through the cooking to distribute the heat evenly.

- For quick roast potatoes, start the cooking in a microwave cooker then brown and crisp them in hot fat or oil in a conventional oven.

- Most vegetables tend to have a crisp texture when cooked. If very soft vegetables are required, use the conventional method of cooking.

Q *How long do fresh vegetables take to cook in the microwave?*

A Follow the chart below for the cooking times. When using this chart add 60 ml (4 tbsp) water unless otherwise stated. The vegetables can be cooked in boil-in-the-bags, plastic containers and polythene bags – pierce the bag before cooking to make sure there is a space for steam to escape.

Vegetable	Quantity	Time on HIGH Setting	Microwave Cooking Technique(s)
Artichoke, globe	1	5–6 mins	*Place* upright in covered dish.
	2	7–8 mins	
	3	11–12 mins	
	4	12–13 mins	
Asparagus	450 g (1 lb)	7–8 mins	*Place* stalks towards the outside of the dish. *Reposition* during cooking.
Aubergine	450 g (1 lb) 0.5 cm (¼ inch) slices	5–6 mins	*Stir* or *shake* after 4 minutes.
Beans, broad	450 g (1 lb)	6–8 mins	*Stir* or *shake* after 3 minutes and test after 5 minutes.

VEGETABLES

Vegetable Cooking Times . . . contd.

Vegetable	Quantity	Time on HIGH Setting	Microwave Cooking Technique(s)
Beans, green	450 g (1 lb) sliced into 2.5 cm (1 inch) lengths	10–13 mins	*Stir* or *shake* during the cooking period. Time will vary with age.
Beetroot, whole	4 medium	14–16 mins	*Pierce* skin with a fork. *Reposition* during cooking.
Broccoli	450 g (1 lb) small florets	7–8 mins	*Reposition* during cooking. *Place* stalks towards the outside of the dish.
Brussels sprouts	225 g (8 oz) 450 g (1 lb)	4–6 mins 7–10 mins	*Stir* or *shake* during cooking.
Cabbage	450 g (1 lb) quartered 450 g (1 lb) shredded	8 mins 8–10 mins	*Stir* or *shake* during cooking.
Carrots	450 g (1 lb) small whole 450 g (1 lb) 0.5 cm (¼ inch) slices	8–10 mins 9–12 mins	*Stir* or *shake* during cooking.
Cauliflower	whole 450 g (1 lb) 225 g (8 oz) florets 450 g (1 lb) florets	9–12 mins 5–6 mins 7–8 mins	*Stir* or *shake* during cooking.
Celery	450 g (1 lb) sliced into 2.5 cm (1 inch) lengths	8–10 mins	*Stir* or *shake* during cooking.
Corn-on-the-cob	2 cobs 450 g (1 lb)	6–7 mins	*Wrap* individually in greased greaseproof paper. *Do not* add water. *Turn* over after 3 minutes.

Vegetable Cooking Times ... contd.

Vegetable	Quantity	Time on HIGH Setting	Microwave Cooking Technique(s)
Courgettes	450 g (1 lb) 2.5 cm (1 inch) slices	5–7 mins	*Do not* add more than 30 ml (2 tbsp) water. *Stir* or *shake* gently twice during cooking. *Stand* for 2 minutes before draining.
Fennel	450 g (1 lb)	7–9 mins	*Stir* or *shake* during cooking.
Leeks	0.5 cm (¼ inch) slices 450 g (1 lb) 2.5 cm (1 inch) slices	6–8 mins	*Stir* or *shake* during cooking.
Mangetout	450 g (1 lb)	7–9 mins	*Stir* or *shake* during cooking.
Mushrooms	225 g (8 oz) whole 450 g (1 lb) whole	2–3 mins 5 mins	*Do not* add water. Add 25 g (1 oz) butter or alternative fat and a squeeze of lemon juice. *Stir* or *shake* gently during cooking.
Onions	225 g (8 oz) thinly sliced 450 g (1 lb) small whole	7–8 mins 9–11 mins	*Stir* or *shake* sliced onions. *Add only* 60 ml (4 tbsp) water to whole onions. *Reposition* whole onions during cooking.
Okra	450 g (1 lb) whole	6–8 mins	*Stir* or *shake* during cooking.
Parsnips	450 g (1 lb) halved	10–16 mins	*Place* thinner parts towards the centre. *Add* a knob of butter and 15 ml (1 tbsp) lemon juice with 150 ml (¼ pint) water. *Turn* dish during cooking and *reposition*.
Peas	450 g (1 lb)	9–11 mins	*Stir* or *shake* during cooking.

VEGETABLES

Vegetable Cooking Times ... contd.

Vegetable	Quantity	Time on HIGH Setting	Microwave Cooking Technique(s)
Potatoes			
Baked jacket	1 × 175 g (6 oz) potato	4–6 mins	*Wash* and prick the skin with a fork. *Place* on absorbent kitchen paper or napkin. *When* cooking more than two at a time arrange in a circle. *Turn* over halfway through cooking.
	2 × 175 g (6 oz) potatoes	6–8 mins	
	4 × 175 g (6 oz) potatoes	12–14 mins	
Boiled (old) halved	450 g (1 lb)	7–10 mins	*Add* 60 ml (4 tbsp) water. *Stir* or *shake* during cooking.
Boiled (new) whole	450 g (1 lb)	6–9 mins	*Add* 60 ml (4 tbsp) water. *Do not* overcook or new potatoes become spongy.
Sweet	450 g (1 lb)	5 mins	*Wash* and prick the skin with a fork. *Place* on absorbent kitchen paper. *Turn* over halfway through cooking time.
Spinach	450 g (1 lb) chopped	5–6 mins	*Do not* add water. Best cooked in roasting bag, sealed with non-metal fastening. *Stir* or *shake* during cooking.
Swede	450 g (1 lb) 2 cm (¾ inch) dice	11–13 mins	*Stir* or *shake* during cooking.
Turnip	450 g (1 lb) 2 cm (¾ inch) dice	9–11 mins	*Add* 60 ml (4 tbsp) water and *stir* or *shake* during cooking.

Q *How long should I cook frozen vegetables in the microwave?*

A Follow the times below. They may be cooked straight from the freezer. Many may be cooked in their original plastic packaging, as long as it is first slit and then placed on a plate. Alternatively, transfer to a bowl.

Vegetable	Quantity	Time on HIGH Setting	Microwave Cooking Technique(s)
Asparagus	275 g (10 oz)	7–9 mins	*Separate* and re-arrange after 3 minutes.
Beans, broad	225 g (8 oz)	7–8 mins	*Stir* or *shake* during cooking period.
Beans, green cut	225 g (8 oz)	6–8 mins	*Stir* or *shake* during cooking period.
Broccoli	275 g (10 oz)	7–9 mins	*Re-arrange* spears after 3 minutes.
Brussels sprouts	225 g (8 oz)	6–8 mins	*Stir* or *shake* during cooking period.
Cauliflower florets	275 g (10 oz)	7–9 mins	*Stir* or *shake* during cooking period.
Carrots	225 g (8 oz)	6–7 mins	*Stir* or *shake* during cooking period.
Corn-on-the-cob	1 2	3–4 mins 6–7 mins	*Do not* add water. Dot with butter, wrap in greaseproof paper.
Mixed vegetables	225 g (8 oz)	5–6 mins	*Stir* or *shake* during cooking period.
Peas	225 g (8 oz)	5–6 mins	*Stir* or *shake* during cooking period.
Peas and carrots	225 g (8 oz)	7–8 mins	*Stir* or *shake* during cooking period.
Spinach, leaf or chopped	275 g (10 oz)	7–9 mins	*Do not* add water. *Stir* or *shake* during cooking period.
Swede and Turnip, diced	225 g (8 oz)	6–7 mins	*Stir* or *shake* during cooking period. *Mash* with butter after standing time.
Sweetcorn	225 g (8 oz)	4–6 mins	*Stir* or *shake* during cooking period.

Q *Can I cook several vegetables at one time in the microwave?*

A Yes, this is possible, but you must select vegetables that have the same cooking time (see the vegetable chart on page 129) and prepare them to the same size. Put the vegetables in separate polythene bags, add 30–60 ml (2–4 tbsp) water and tie the bag loosely with a plastic tie, to allow steam to escape.

Aubergines

Q *Can I cook aubergines in the microwave?*

A Yes, whole aubergines cook beautifully in the microwave. Simply prick the skin all over then rub with a little oil. Place on a piece of absorbent kitchen paper and cook on HIGH. Turn over halfway through cooking. A 450 g (1 lb) aubergine will take 6–10 minutes to cook until soft enough to purée. Reduce the cooking time to about 4–8 minutes if you just want to soften the aubergine for slicing and making into dishes such as moussaka.

Cauliflowers

Q *When I cook cauliflower in the microwave it is never really tender. Can you advise me what to do?*

A Cauliflower is rather difficult to cook evenly in the microwave due to the difference in texture of the florets and stalk. It is therefore best to divide it into florets for even cooking and use the stalks for making soups.

Onions

Q *I often just want to cook a chopped onion until it's soft. Is this possible in the microwave?*

A Yes, this can be very useful. Simply put the oil or butter and the chopped onion in a medium bowl, cover and cook on HIGH, stirring occasionally. (One small onion takes 4–5 minutes until softened; one medium onion takes 5–7 minutes until softened; one large onion takes 7 minutes until softened).

Peppers

Q *Is there an easy way to skin peppers using the microwave?*

A Yes, cut the peppers in half and place cut side down on a plate. Cook on HIGH for about 1 minute per pepper, or until the skin just starts to change colour and peel away. Once cool enough to handle, the peppers will be very easy to skin.

Potatoes

Q *How do I cook jacket potatoes in the microwave?*

A These are probably the most popular choice for microwave cooking because, in small numbers, they can be cooked in a fraction of the time it takes to cook them conventionally. Although their skins are not crisp they make a delicious quick snack. To cook jacket potatoes, scrub the potatoes and prick all over with a fork. Arrange on absorbent kitchen

Arrange potatoes on absorbent kitchen paper.

paper in a circle in the cooker. Cook on HIGH until soft. (1 large potato, weighing about 175 g (6 oz), will take 4–6 minutes; 2 large potatoes will take 6–8 minutes; 4 large potatoes will take 12–14 minutes.)

Q *What is the best way to prepare mashed potato in the microwave?*

A The following method is perhaps the simplest.

4 medium potatoes, each weighing about 175 g (6 oz)
25 g (1 oz) butter or margarine
about 75 ml (5 tbsp) milk
salt and pepper

1 Scrub the potatoes and prick all over with a fork. Arrange on absorbent kitchen paper in a circle in the cooker and cook on HIGH for 12–14 minutes or until tender, turning over once.

2 When the potatoes are cooked, remove from the cooker and set aside to cool slightly. Peel the potatoes and put in a bowl. Add the butter or margarine and enough milk to make a soft mashed potato. Mash together thoroughly. Season to taste with salt and pepper.

Q *When I have conventionally boiled potatoes, drained them and turned them into a bowl for mashing, I often come across one or two that are still hard. Can I finish cooking them in the microwave?*

A Yes, the microwave excels at helping with this sort of cookery problem. Simply leave all of the potatoes in the bowl, add milk and butter as usual, then mash as much as possible. Cover the bowl with a plate, then cook on HIGH for 3–4 minutes. You will find that all of the potatoes are now soft enough to mash.

W

WATER

Q *Can I boil water in the microwave?*

A Yes. Put the water in a jug or bowl and place in the cooker. Set on HIGH. If you require more than 300 ml (½ pint) water, however, then it will be quicker and more economical to boil the water in an electric kettle.

INDEX